ENDORSEME|

The Word of God is prophetically and painfully obvious when you look at the headlines today. The body of Christ needs a profound change in their understanding of the effectiveness of our impact. We must be willing to readjust our methods and completely change our wineskins. Alan DiDio brings an understanding of the realities of what is going on around us and gives us information on how to meet this acceleration head-on without compromising our moral and ethical responsibilities.

Using the Word of God, this book helps you grasp the truth of the fallen world we live in today. If the body of Christ thinks that they are going to get through this day without understanding what the Word of God says about end-time theology, thinking it is just pie in the sky and that whole thing about Jesus coming back is ridiculous, then I want to tell you NO! This is basic Christianity, and we have got to get back to the Word of God.

This book helps you navigate the advancement of technology, focusing on AI and the great deception and what nephilim, aliens, and skinwalkers have in common. This book will shine a light on satan's end-time strategy and how all these topics were prophesied from the beginning of time and found throughout the Bible.

Troy A. Brewer
Senior Pastor of OpenDoor Church in Burleson, Texas
Author of *31 Battle Cry Declarations, Redeeming Your Timeline,*
Numbers That Preach, Good Overcomes Evil, Looking Up,
and *Soul Invasion*
TroyBrewer.com | ODX.tv

2 Thessalonians 2:7 says, *"For the mystery of lawlessness is already at work…"* If there is an invisible force warring against us, shouldn't we know it? And shouldn't we understand the objective of that force? But most of all, shouldn't we assume our role in defeating it? *Summoning the Demon* is the best analysis of the weapons, tactics, and people satan is using to dominate the world. Learn how to prepare. Learn how to be victorious.

Mario Murillo
Living Proof

My friend Alan DiDio is one of the great communicators of our day. As I read *Summoning the Demon*, I am compelled to say that the reader can rest assured Alan has done his homework! *Summoning the Demon* is well-written and enjoyable to read; it is informative, documented, and packed with clear information about these vital issues—prophetically speaking, it is indeed a NOW WORD!

I found myself highly engaged by the insights throughout this entire book. From start to finish, each page was gripping! Segments where Alan compares the nuclear bomb to our modern-day AI to the very end are loaded with powerful, real-world insights. He masterfully deals with the rising technological storm, UFOs, issues such as Project Blue Beam, Blue Book, Skinwalker Ranch and other paranormal scenarios, the coming of the antichrist, and so much more while offering helpful explanations and a sound biblical foundation.

Although it would appear that the world's system is on the path of forfeiting its position to technology as the "dominant species" on earth, as well as allowing many other forms of evil to cascade directly at society—we can take refuge in knowing we have mighty promises to stand on as a defense against these dark clouds rising.

Many of the insights offered in this well-written book are mind-blowing! What I found to be very refreshing is Alan's scriptural paint-by-numbers response to many of these coming issues while offering answers to vital questions you may not have known how to ask. Information that brings peace is a must as we stare down the barrel of the world we now find ourselves in. Regardless of the challenges we face, you will discover that the Ekklesia or the Church of Jesus Christ restrains the worst of what is to come! Much of the conclusions found here will cause rejoicing in the heart of the reader!

Alan's latest book is a MUST-READ for anyone who wishes to be informed and armed with a faith-filled hope for the future. This book will weaponize your faith and make you very hazardous to the kingdom of darkness! To Alan, I want to say well done, my friend!

Joseph Z
Author, Broadcaster, Prophetic Voice | JosephZ.com

Summoning the Demon bridges the gap between cutting-edge AI technology, biblical prophecy, and the supernatural, offering an essential read for anyone interested in the intersection of faith and science. As a Christian who's been looking at these fringe topics for nearly a decade, I find this book to be a treasure trove of insights into the ethical and spiritual dimensions of aliens and artificial intelligence.

Tony Merkel
The Confessionals

In *Summoning the Demon*, Pastor Alan DiDio brilliantly navigates the complex intersection of advanced technology, possible extraterrestrial phenomena, and eschatological themes. In an era where the lines between reality and science fiction are increasingly blurred, this book emerges as a critical guide for believers to navigate the data and facts. Pastor DiDio not only explores, but also demystifies how these elements are interwoven with the Bible and our Christian faith, providing a much-needed theological perspective.

As we face unprecedented advancements in technology and growing curiosity about extraterrestrial life, it's imperative for believers to have a grounded understanding of these issues in light of Scripture. This book does precisely that, equipping readers with knowledge and wisdom to discern the signs of the times.

Furthermore, this book is a clarion call for the Christian community at this late hour in human history. It urges believers to be vigilant, informed, and spiritually prepared as we navigate these complex topics in a world that is rapidly evolving and often challenging the core tenets of our faith.

This is not just a book; it's a necessary tool for every believer seeking to contend for the faith in an increasingly complex and challenging world. *Summoning the Demon* is a must-read, serving as both an eye-opener and a beacon of hope, reminding us of the power of our faith in Jesus Christ amidst a rapidly changing global landscape.

Pastor Todd Coconato
President and Host, Todd Coconato Ministries
Todd Coconato Radio Show | Religious Liberty Coalition

Only Alan DiDio has the guts to take conspiracy theories whispered in the corners of society and prove they are, in fact, reality. Not to mention backing up his statements with in-depth scripture. The shocking topics discussed in *Summoning the Demon* need to be exposed. Since I have personally come in contact with alien beings and the demons behind them, I understand the insidious agenda they are working against believers and the people of the world mentally, physically, socially, economically, and in our government spheres. Unless the church wakes up and learns how to be armed to destroy these strategies, we all may be in extraordinary peril.

Katie Souza
Host, Faith with Katie | www.KatieSouza.com

SUMMONING
THE Demon

SUMMONING
THE Demon

AI
ALIENS
& THE
ANTICHRIST

ALAN DIDIO

DESTINY IMAGE® PUBLISHERS, INC.
P.O. Box 310, Shippensburg, PA 17257-0310

"Publishing cutting-edge prophetic resources to supernaturally empower the body of Christ"

This book and all other Destiny Image and Destiny Image Fiction books are available at Christian bookstores and distributors worldwide.

For more information on foreign distributors, call 717-532-3040.

Reach us on the Internet: www.destinyimage.com.

ISBN 13 TP: 978-0-7684-7968-3

ISBN 13 eBook: 978-0-7684-7969-0

For Worldwide Distribution, Printed in the U.S.A.

1 2 3 4 5 6 7 8 / 28 27 26 25 24

CONTENTS

FOREWORD

Without question, *Summoning the Demon* is among the most brilliant and intelligent books I have read on subjects related to the end times. In this work, Alan DiDio rightly declares that the road before us is laden with peril, but we are not without a compass or a guide because we have the Word of God to guide us along the way. But then he goes a step further, forging into some of the most important issues to confront us in the present and in the times to come, including AI, genetic engineering, UFO-based religions, and the rise of the antichrist, among many other issues. Through it all, Alan shows us what the correct Christian response should be.

Alan writes about the need to break the grip of supernatural deception and the need for the Church to provide clarity, instruction, and truth from the Bible on these confrontational issues. And clarity, instruction, and truth is precisely what is provided in this remarkable book! The author intelligently states that we must respond to these troubling times with faith rather than fear, wisdom rather than awe, and compassion rather than curiosity. He further expresses that in a world full of dark corners and delusions, believers must be salt and light, and that in this time when the truth is frequently distorted and obscured, we must be staunch bearers of this truth.

I must honestly state that this book is so fabulous, I wish I had written it! But I did not, so it is my amazing privilege to endorse it with the highest possible recommendation. This is not a book to purchase and leave on your bookshelf unread. Read it, devour it, and open your mind to all these pages describe that will confront us as we race to the conclusion of the age.

Rick Renner
Minister, Author, Broadcaster
Moscow, Russia

AI AND THE GREAT DECEPTION

Is Artificial Intelligence (AI) in Bible prophecy?

Will the antichrist use AI to take power in this generation?

Elon Musk, one of the most powerful personalities in the world of technology, paused for a moment of reflection as he sat before an auditorium filled with people. He took a long, deep breath before making this profoundly prophetic statement:

> "With AI, we are summoning the demon."[1]

When I heard this quote myself, it felt less like a metaphor and more like a prophetic utterance. This technological genius, who does not profess to be a Christian, compared artificial intelligence to "summoning the demon," and went on to suggest that we might be conjuring something that we think we can control, only to find out that it will turn against us.

> "The development of AI could spell the end of the human race."
>
> **—Stephen Hawking**[2]

These statements serve as a disturbing reminder of the potential pandora's box that has already been opened. We are now burdened with the responsibility of heeding this warning and exercising judgment as we stand on the brink of a brave new world. During times of great darkness, it is not uncommon for the Church to bury its head in the sand and hope that the storm will blow over. However, we cannot risk letting others seize control of the levers of power—the stakes are too high. We must not remain ignorant or uninfluential in this AI arms race.

Much like the scientists who worked on the Manhattan Project, AI research centers around the world are trying to understand the implications of what's being created. They are working on developing artificial general intelligence (AGI), which refers to robots or programs that are able to acquire and grasp any intellectual endeavor that a human being is capable of, but with exponentially greater efficiency and capacity.

Many experts fear we are approaching a *technological singularity*: a hypothetical future point in time at which technological growth becomes uncontrollable and irreversible, resulting in unforeseeable changes to human civilization.[3]

The term *singularity* is also used to describe what happens when you cross the threshold into a black hole. All of the known laws of nature break down or even disappear. Sound mystical? It should! This is the realm we're stepping into with AI. With each breakthrough and advancement, the boundaries of human achievement expand, blurring the line between science fiction and reality.

ARE WE CREATING A MODERN-DAY GOLEM?

The golem, a creature deeply rooted in mystical Jewish folklore and mythology, has long captured the imagination of believers and skeptics alike. The origins of this belief can be traced back to ancient Jewish texts, which gradually gained prominence during the Middle Ages. Legend has it that the golem, a creature fashioned from clay or mud, was said to have been animated through enigmatic rituals and inscriptions. The creation of such artifacts was traditionally entrusted to esteemed rabbis or mystics who possessed deep knowledge and understanding of the sacred name of God.

This demonic portrayal of the golem as a formidable but devoid-of-thought servant, dutifully following the commands of its maker, is both captivating and unsettling. The primary objective for this creature was to safeguard and shield the Jewish community from imminent threats and relentless persecution. In certain renditions of the ancient legend, the golem is said to have been conjured forth in moments of dire peril and turmoil, assuming the role of a stalwart protector against adversaries and tyrants. We've even seen parallels of this in movies like *Avengers: Age of Ultron* where Tony Stark attempts to protect the world but ends up threatening it with the creation of an out-of-control AI.

Nevertheless, the golem's remarkable strength coupled with its dearth of human intellect presented a perilous predicament. In the absence of adequate control or limitations, the golem possesses the potential to spiral into an uncontrollable force, unleashing catastrophic havoc upon its surroundings. The narrative surrounding the golem delves into profound themes of authority, accountability, and the ethical ramifications inherent in assuming the role of a deity.

AGI possesses a similar threat as the golem and even the atomic bomb. These are comparisons that top tech executives are making. If artificial intelligence were to get into the wrong hands or to get out of control, the repercussions may be catastrophic, far exceeding the harm that could be caused by a bomb or a mythical monster. The development of this kind of AI could result in:

- Economic disparities on a scale never seen before.
- The loss of the right to privacy with mass surveillance.
- Deepfake scams that defrauded both individuals and nations.
- Unprecedented national security breaches.
- Election engineering.
- The complete breakdown of interpersonal relationships in society.
- The collapse of how we define reality.
- The hacking of the human mind.
- Or a dystopian future in which humans are no longer the dominant species.

The last one may seem like a stretch but in a recent survey of 4,000 AI researchers, nearly half of them acknowledged that they believed there was a ten percent chance that this tech could result in human extinction. That's not very comforting.

WHAT DOES THE BIBLE SAY ABOUT AI?

> But thou, O Daniel, shut up the words, and seal the book, even to the time of the end: many shall run to and fro, and knowledge shall be increased (Daniel 12:4 KJV).

Is Daniel predicting an explosion of knowledge? If so, we are sitting right in the middle of the fulfillment of this prophecy! Consider this:

- In the 1950s, knowledge was doubling every 20-30 years. Today, knowledge is doubling every 15 months.

- Your phone has more tech on it than the first space shuttle.

- The average newspaper today has more information than the average person living in the 17th century would come across in their lifetime.

During this knowledge explosion, the Bible speaks of a coming figure who will seek to dominate the world and will perpetuate the greatest deception known to man. The antichrist will attempt to seize the reins of power by specifically controlling the world economy. For centuries there has been a great deal of speculation as to how he would be able to accomplish this. How could someone control who buys and sells *and* how would one monitor this? Today the answer is simple: a digital currency with a powerful AI superintending over it.

> *And he had power to give life unto the image of the beast, that the image of the beast should both speak, and cause that as many as would not worship the image of the beast should be killed* (Revelation 13:15 KJV).

Here the Bible says that this end-time leader will possess an "image," icon, or idol that he will "give life" to. Could this be a reference to an automaton powered by a demonically inspired AI?

It's interesting to also note that the first characteristic of the image is that it could "speak." The breakthroughs that we have seen in recent months are in the area of AI language models. Everyone is shocked at how it's able to speak and some are even asserting sentience.

HOW SHOULD THE CHURCH RESPOND?

Recently a Lutheran church in Germany hosted an AI worship service with four different AI ministers. The sermon lasted about 40 minutes and hundreds lined up to hear it. Though we should not be running to line up and hear an AI preacher, we should also not be running from the technology we've seen so far. We need to be as involved as we can be in this process. We must pray that within these tech companies, God will raise up some spirit-filled programmers to insert truth into these algorithms. We should also help train these modules by using them and inputting as much Gospel as we can.

Understanding AI is part of the end-time stewardship Jesus commissioned us to walk in. We must help to ensure, to the best of our ability, that such powerful tools are used ethically and responsibly.

We're not in the antichrist system yet, but it is fast approaching. The scaffolding for the great deception is already in place. Some have suggested that we will cross over into the technological singularity by 2045. Others think we could have AGI within the next two years. Ultimately, believers must be ready.

> Watch ye therefore, and pray always, that ye may be accounted worthy to escape all these things that shall come to pass, and to stand before the Son of man (Luke 21:36 KJV).

These are exciting times! As we see these prophecies being fulfilled, we must see them as an invitation to engage the world around us, increase our influence for the kingdom, and "occupy till He comes" (see Luke 19:13). Maranatha!

- Is it already too late or can we still have an impact?

- Did the Bible predict AI?
- How does this tie into current UFO and alien phenomena?
- Does the Bible speak about UFOs and alien entities?
- Who is the antichrist and why should it matter to the average Christian?
- What role will all this play in the antichrist agenda?

In this book, we will answer these questions, and we will also examine issues such as:

- Are aliens or UFOs mentioned in the Bible?
- Who are the Nephilim?
- Can we trust extra-biblical sources like the Book of Enoch?
- How do these subjects align with other "conspiracy theories"?

As we venture closer and closer to the Lord's return, we must be able to speak to these issues. Hosea 4:6 says that God's people are destroyed by a lack of knowledge. Destruction is knocking at the door, and you and I must understand our role in these last days. Jesus is coming—and greater is He that is in you than He that is in the world. We can still turn this world upside down for His glory if we are ready to give an answer for the hope that lies within us.

CHAPTER ONE

THE MANHATTAN PROJECT:
Birth of a New Era

"The release of atom power has changed everything except our way of thinking...the solution to this problem lies in the heart of mankind. If only I had known, I should have become a watchmaker."
—Albert Einstein[4]

"Behold, I have created the smith that bloweth the coals in the fire, and that bringeth forth an instrument for his work; and I have created the waster to destroy."
—Isaiah 54:16 KJV

Underneath the desert skies of Los Alamos, New Mexico, a select group of specialists toiled over an idea that was capable of creating both peace and death: the Manhattan Project. As they huddled together over their work, the ticking of the clock served as punctuation for each moment of contemplative silence. They were on the verge of making a discovery that would irrevocably alter the course of human history.

The year was 1942. The Allies were suffering defeat as World War II continued to rage on. The Germans had created a new weapon, the V-2 rocket, which was wreaking havoc in London and bringing death and destruction with it. The Allies were concerned that the Germans were also working on the development of an atomic weapon, and they recognized the urgency of the situation.

Under the direction of J. Robert Oppenheimer, these individuals were pioneers who were venturing into the uncharted territory of atomic power. Like Adam and Eve in Genesis 3, they were faced with a choice that bore tremendous moral weight. Either they could retain the status quo and allow the catastrophic power of the atom to remain untapped, or they could take a bite out of the apple of nuclear knowledge, which would permanently change the world. Had they waited, the enemy could have acquired this devastating knowledge first and destroyed everything they held dear.

One day, a young researcher by the name of Leo Szilard made a significant discovery. He came to the conclusion that an atomic weapon could be manufactured through the utilization of a nuclear chain reaction. This was the most important step in the process of constructing a bomb that was large enough to put an end to the war. They were up against a tight deadline, and they were well aware that the Germans were not far behind them. Finally, on July 16, 1945, they were successful. In the middle of the New Mexico desert, they detonated the first atomic bomb.

The explosion caused a blinding flash of light and a boom that could only be described as ear-splitting. As the mushroom cloud climbed higher into the sky, the heat was so intense that it vaporized everything that was within a mile of where the detonation occurred.

The Manhattan Project was a success, but it was accomplished at a significant cost. The researchers who worked on the project were

The "Fat Man" pictured here was the kind of nuclear weapon detonated over Nagasaki, Japan, in World War II. The bomb is 60 inches in diameter and 128 inches long. The second nuclear weapon to be detonated, weighed about 10,000 pounds and had a yield equivalent of approximately 20,000 tons of high explosive.

Credit: Los Alamos Scientific Laboratory, National Archives

troubled by the notion that they were responsible for the development of a weapon designed to cause widespread harm. They were aware that the bomb had the potential to cause the deaths of millions of people, and they dreaded the possibility that it would be used in that way.

Later, when reflecting on his experience, Robert Oppenheimer cited a passage from the Bhagavad Gita (Hindu scripture), saying, "Now I am become Death, the destroyer of worlds."[5] This unsettling sentiment echoed the dichotomy of their creation, which was a tool of unrivaled destruction but was also the means by which a world war was ended.

A dense column of smoke rises more than 60,000 feet into the air over the Japanese port of Nagasaki, the result of an atomic bomb, the second ever used in warfare, dropped on the industrial center August 9, 1945, from a U.S. B-29 Superfortress.

Credit: National Archives and Records Administration

HERE WE GO AGAIN

Let's jump ahead in time to the beginning of the 21st century. The test sites of artificial intelligence research centers all around the world have a similar dilemma. These AI researchers, just like the scientists who worked on the Manhattan Project, are trying to understand the implications of what they are creating. They are working on developing artificial general intelligence (AGI), which refers to robots that are able to acquire and grasp any intellectual endeavor that a human being is capable of, but with exponentially greater efficiency and capacity. Let's revisit the concept of a technological singularity again—that hypothetical future tipping point of technological advancement.

The creation of AGI (or AI, as we'll call its various forms throughout this book) is a game-changer, much like the atomic bomb. If artificial intelligence were to get into the wrong hands or to get out of control, the repercussions could be catastrophic, far exceeding the harm that could be caused by a nuclear bomb. As I mentioned, it could result in economic disparities on a scale never seen before, a loss of individuals' right to privacy, or even a dystopian future in which humans are no longer the dominant species.

Artificial intelligence also has the potential to accomplish a great deal of good in the world. It could lead to scientific breakthroughs, provide solutions to difficult problems, and even assist us in better understanding our own thinking. The development of AI may potentially one day lead to the elimination of cancer. Consider Genesis 11:6 (KJV):

> Behold, the people is one, and they have all one language; and this they begin to do: and now nothing will be restrained from them, which they have imagined to do.

In other words, nothing will stop them from doing whatever it is that they have imagined doing. This verse can be interpreted as a warning about human ambition, which is pertinent to both the development of artificial intelligence and the Manhattan Project. Are we, as a society, ready to wield the power we are rapidly unlocking? It seems that few in the industry itself are willing to pause, even for a moment, to answer that question. Besides, if we stop, perhaps our enemies will get there first. We are in an AI arms race!

A significant dilemma lies at the center of both of these historic moments. As we get closer and closer to replicating and possibly surpassing our own intelligence, are we playing god by doing so, or are we only fulfilling the potential that He has given us?

THE GENESIS OF AI: A NEW FRONTIER

In the beginning was the Word, and the Word was with God, and the Word was God (John 1:1 KJV).

Alan Turing, a mathematician who was decades ahead of his time, had a vision in the aftermath of World War II that would change the way we view ourselves in the world. In the 1950s, Turing was envisioning how humanity's future would play out. Turing planted the initial seeds of a concept that would eventually give rise to a new world in the winding passageways of Bletchley Park, surrounded by the lingering smell of burnt wiring and oil. This idea was artificial intelligence.

Imagine a solitary figure hunched over his cluttered desk under a dim, flickering light, his eyes locked onto an old, weathered notebook. Guided by a revolutionary thought, he began sketching out his ideas about how a machine might mimic the human mind. Little did he know then that his humble hypotheses would spur a field of study with the potential to outstrip human intelligence.

The question was: "Can machines think?" This straightforward inquiry posed by Turing sparked a complex web of ethical and moral debates. Turing was so intrigued by the possibility of human-like intelligence in robots that he developed a test to help know when we've passed that threshold. It's called, aptly, "The Turing Test."[6]

During the evaluation, a human interrogator uses normal language to have discussions with both another human and a computer that is supposed to generate responses that are similar to those of actual people. The primary objective of the system is to create the impression in the mind of the evaluator, solely on the basis of the discussion, that they are having the conversation with another human person. The machine is considered to have successfully completed the evaluation if the evaluator is unable to distinguish between the machine and the human in a reliable manner.

I asked ChatGPT if it could pass the Turing Test. Here was its response:

> As an AI language model, I'm designed to generate responses that are as human-like as possible, and many people find these responses convincing. However, the Turing Test is a complex challenge that includes not only producing human-like text, but also understanding and responding to a broad range of human emotions, subtleties, idioms, and cultural references, among other things. While I can handle many of these aspects to some extent, there are likely to be cases where my responses may not be entirely indistinguishable from those of a human.

> Additionally, a major aspect of the Turing Test is the ability to exhibit understanding and intentionality—the capacity to understand the meanings of words, to refer to things in the world, and to have beliefs, desires, and intentions. As an AI, I don't possess beliefs, desires, or consciousness. I generate responses based on patterns and information in the data I was trained on, without any understanding or intentionality.
>
> So, while I aim to provide helpful, accurate, and human-like responses, there are important respects in which I wouldn't be able to fully pass the Turing Test, especially if the test includes a deep or broad range of conversational contexts.[7]

Here's a question: would AI tell us if it did develop consciousness? Additionally, there are a few well-known examples of machines that have made an effort to pass the Turing Test:

- **ELIZA**: Named after Eliza Doolittle, a character from George Bernard Shaw's play *Pygmalion,* later adapted as the classic movie *My Fair Lady.* ELIZA was a piece of software, developed in the 1960s, that emulates the work of a Rogerian psychotherapist. ELIZA was able to pass the Turing Test with some success, but in the end, it was discovered that the program was just a straightforward pattern-matching algorithm.[8]

- **PARRY**: A computer program called PARRY, developed in the 1970s, mimicked the mental state of a paranoid schizo-phrenic. Unlike ELIZA, PARRY was successful in passing the Turing Test, but in the end, it was discovered to be nothing more than software that was obeying a predetermined set of instructions.[9]

- **EUGENE GOOSTMAN**: A chatbot named Eugene Goostman was built in Ukraine. It pretended to be a boy from the Crimean peninsula who was 13 years old. Eugene Goostman successfully passed the Turing Test in a competition in 2014. However, it was later discovered that the software was actually being operated by a human being behind the scenes.

- **LaMDA**: In 2022, Google's AI language model, LaMDA, was reported to have passed the Turing Test. However, this claim was disputed by some experts, who argued that the test was not conducted fairly.[10]

You can take that for what it's worth. As advanced as many different AI chatbots may be, it's obvious that we're not there yet, but this doesn't mean that it's not fast approaching. We must answer these moral dilemmas now before we cross that threshold and it's too late.

With chatbot tech becoming the newest craze, personal security will quickly become a priority. There is AI in existence today that can take a 60 second recording of your voice and replicate it perfectly. Imagine your wife getting a call and thinking it's from you saying you're at the doctor and you need your social security number.

Again, these moral issues are similar to those with which the scientists working on the Manhattan Project had to grapple. However, rather than harnessing the raw destructive potential of the atom, these many pioneers are trying to imitate the complexity of the human mind. The results will be even more transformative, if not catastrophic.

In the same way that Oppenheimer and his team struggled to come to terms with the devastating potential of their invention, the creators of AI must come to terms with the ethical consequences of their work:

- What exactly does it mean to develop a consciousness that is not human?
- Is it morally acceptable?
- What legal protections should a sentient AI have?

As with the atomic bomb, what safeguards can we put in place to prevent this potent invention from being abused or getting into the wrong hands?

There is currently vigorous discussion that surrounds these concerns. In the pursuit of artificial general intelligence, academics and scientists are at odds over the ramifications, which go beyond the area of technology and reach into the social, economic, philosophical, and religious spheres. One might even say that many scientists are sounding more like theologians than inventors—and bad theologians at that: "*ever learning, and never able to come to the knowledge of the truth*" (2 Timothy 3:7 KJV).

Elon Musk has repeatedly made it clear that he considers AI to be one of the most significant existential threats to humanity if it is not properly managed and regulated, and he has made repeated calls for more stringent and aggressive regulation in this area. He and others have been particularly vocal about the dangers that are posed by highly sophisticated AI, which could, in theory, execute every intellectual work that a human being is capable of doing.

I predict that as people become more attached to these "bots," society will redefine consciousness to include AI in a demented attempt to be "tolerant" of a new definition of love.

Are we standing at the edge of an abyss or on the cusp of a new frontier? Those who have read their Bible know the ultimate answer to that question.

As we venture deeper into the uncharted territory of artificial intelligence, we must not forget the lessons of the past. The Manhattan Project is a sobering illustration of the ease with which power may be abused, and the extent to which it can cause devastation when it is. To help you better grasp the profundity of this moment, I've placed the statement released by the President announcing the use of the A-bomb at Hiroshima in Appendix A of this book. Be sure to read it and allow its sobriety to grip you.

We do not yet understand all the ramifications of the developing field of artificial intelligence. However, there is one thing that can be said for certain: satan is already making efforts—and this is not the first time he has done so—to appropriate this technology for his own ends. In the next chapter, we will take a look back in time, and if we're lucky, we'll discover some answers to the questions we have about the future in the past.

CHAPTER TWO

AI AND THE TOWER OF BABEL

*"Language as the technology of human extension, whose
powers of division and separation we know so well, may
have been the 'Tower of Babel' by which men sought
to scale the highest heavens. Today computers hold out
the promise of a means of instant translation of any
code or language into any other code or language."*
—Marshall McLuhan[11]

*"For we wrestle not against flesh and blood, but
against principalities, against powers, against
the rulers of the darkness of this world, against
spiritual wickedness in high places."*
—Ephesians 6:12 KJV

ASPIRING FOR THE HEAVENS

In the heart of Mesopotamia, under a sky filled with foreboding
storm clouds, the most audacious project of the ancient world was
taking shape. King Nimrod, a figure of legend and power, had galva-
nized the people of Babel. Their collective ambition was reflected in
a monolithic tower rising defiantly against the heavens—a testament

to human unity and determination. The echoes of hammering and chiseling drowned the murmurs of discontent and fear.

Some whispered that they were challenging the gods; others worried that they were digging their own graves. Yet, no one wanted to defy Nimrod the great hunter. His name and his reputation speak of an evil ruler who specialized in hunting men and consuming them. In some traditions, sacrificial cannibalism and contact with fallen angels aided his rise to power. Were they building a tower to the literal heavens or were they opening a portal to communicate with demonic entities? Nimrod was undeterred. He saw this tower, this magnificent symbol of human achievement, as the means to etch his name into the annals of eternity.

Some speculate that under Nimrod's rule, humankind harnessed technology beyond the comprehension of the age, from advanced construction techniques to possible genetic manipulation. These theories, while speculative, depict a society striving to transcend their human limitations.

Others suggest that the construction of such an edifice necessitated a fundamental grasp of architectural principles such as the distribution of weight and the use of angular structures for stability. It's possible that they harnessed rudimentary forms of machinery, utilizing pulley systems and inclined planes, to aid in the movement and placement of large building blocks. Even now, we're unable to grasp how many of the ancient structures were created.

With such thoughts in mind, it is not hard to understand why God intervened in this enterprise. Nimrod, in utter defiance of the sovereignty of God, had declared that he would build a tower so high that it would reach into the heavens. The Lord God knew that with the support of his workforce and with the knowledge he had gained, Nimrod would indeed achieve his goal. In effect, what he was saying was, "I will be able to come and go as I please into the heavens where God dwells, and I will be equal with God."

This sentiment is strikingly familiar to the one made by lucifer before he fell:

> I will ascend above the heights of the clouds; I will be like the most High (Isaiah 14:14 KJV).

Nimrod had to be stopped, and he was. He was denied unlawful entrance into the heavens. Lucifer was cast from the presence of God; Nimrod was prevented from entering into the presence of God "*above the heights of the clouds.*"

A LEAP BEYOND TIME: THE FORBIDDEN KNOWLEDGE OF BABEL

Stepping into the realm of the speculative, some theories suggest that Nimrod and his society were privy to knowledge and technology imparted by supernatural or demonic entities. It is a chilling thought that sends shivers down the spine and expands our understanding of the Babel era. One such theory suggests that Nimrod's society had mastered the manipulation of frequencies. Even today, the power of frequency manipulation is evident in a multitude of technologies, from telecommunications and radio broadcasts to advanced medical imaging techniques. In the hands of a Babel society, it could have been used in ways we can barely imagine.

It has been proposed that they harnessed sonic resonance to aid in the construction of the Tower of Babel. By tuning into the natural resonance frequencies of the stone blocks, they could theoretically cause them to vibrate and levitate, allowing them to be moved and positioned with minimal effort. This theory, though abstract, draws upon principles of acoustics and vibration that we are only beginning to fully appreciate in the modern era. Will AI allow us to tap into these lost technologies?

The concept of frequency manipulation extends beyond mere construction and into the realm of mind control and influence. Today, we understand that certain frequencies can induce different mental states, from calmness and relaxation to anxiety and agitation. Could it be that Nimrod's society used similar techniques to maintain control over the masses, ensuring obedience to their grand project?

Perhaps the most sinister theory suggests that this knowledge wasn't the result of human ingenuity but had been imparted by demonic forces. The Bible tells us of fallen angels, entities cast out from heaven, who interfered with human affairs. These entities, known by some as the Watchers, are said to have taught humans forbidden knowledge, which included, according to one questionable ancient text, "sorceries, and incantations, and the dividing of roots and trees."[12]

Perhaps Nimrod, known for his defiance of God, had allied with these entities to gain access to their forbidden knowledge? Beyond these architectural marvels, some theories delve into the realm of genetics. The Book of Genesis tells us about a race of giants that once walked the Earth:

> *There were giants in the earth in those days; and also after that, when the sons of God came in unto the daughters of men, and they bare children to them, the same became mighty men which were of old, men of renown* (Genesis 6:4 KJV).

Is it possible that this alliance might have included insights into genetic manipulation, leading to the creation of the Nephilim (more on this later), and the advanced technology supposedly evident in Babel? These theories suggest that through some unknown means, they had the capacity to alter or influence genetic characteristics, leading to the rise of supernatural technological advancements. While this idea is hypothetical, it paints a picture of an ancient society daringly innovative and pushing the boundaries of their understanding by means of communing with fallen angels.

Despite the centuries that separate us from the Babel era, we stand upon a similar precipice of scientific and technological breakthroughs.

Just as the people of Babel under Nimrod's rule strove to reach the heavens, AI developers today seek to create a god-like machine that will embody supreme knowledge and intelligence. Is this aspiration a symbol of our collective progress and ingenuity? Or are we, like the people of Babel, defying the natural order and overreaching our bounds?

The parallel between Nimrod and the antichrist in biblical prophecy is a compelling one. Both are depicted as charismatic leaders wielding tremendous power, leading their followers toward a vision that ultimately challenges the divine order. While Nimrod sought to build a tower that reached the heavens, the antichrist, as prophesied, will seek to establish dominion over all of mankind—possibly with the aid of advanced technologies such as AI.

The Tower of Babel stands as a testament to the potential dangers of unchecked ambition and the pursuit of knowledge without wisdom or restraint. Genesis 11:6-7 says:

> *And the Lord said, "Behold, they are one people, and they have all one language, and this is only the beginning of what they will do. And nothing that they*

propose to do will now be impossible for them. Come, let us go down and there confuse their language, so that they may not understand one another's speech" (ESV).

Are we, in our pursuit of AI, standing at a similar crossroads? Is our quest to create an artificial superintelligence an echo of the hubris that led to the downfall of Babel? The answer to all these questions is a resounding *yes!* Similarly to those in Genesis 11, those of us who find ourselves in the 21st century are discovering the capabilities of AI that allow us to communicate with others from all over the world in the same language, irrespective of location or nationality. I've personally been on mission trips where I was surrounded by people who spoke a foreign language, but I was able to use AI to translate everything I was saying.

As we forge ahead in our technological advancements, we must ponder these parallels and the lessons they offer. The Tower of Babel warns us of the perils of overreaching ambition. It teaches us to strive for progress but reminds us to temper our ambition with wisdom and humility, ensuring our creations serve to uplift humanity toward Christ, not lead it into chaos and destruction.

Some in the tech industry have called for a pause in the rapid development of AI, but you know as well as I do that no one is listening. China is pushing forward to be the first to break through in this digital "space race," and for-profit companies will not slow down their research.

What can we do? We must become relentless in our evangelism. I'm committed to preaching the Gospel of Jesus Christ in every sphere of influence that He gives me. If we'll be faithful, we can see conspicuous conversions in the lives of those who are developing these technologies.

AI is only as good as the information deposited in it and the prompts it receives. Let's pray that some radical believers will be in positions of power, like Joseph, and drop some Gospel into these systems.

WHAT CAN WE DO ABOUT THE RISE OF AI?

With the ever-increasing availability of digital echo chambers, micro-targeting, the misuse of personal data, and the deterioration of human interaction, this generation is in danger of being easily led astray and controlled by the enemy.

Here are a few pointers on how we can respond to the subtle manipulation of these algorithms and walk in freedom:

1. We must commit to the renewing of our minds, and we must intentionally seek out the washing of the water of the Word of God.

2. We must prioritize in-person, one-on-one discipleship. Not forsaking the assembling of ourselves together and submitting to spiritual authority can go a long way toward promoting healthy relationships and a strong spiritual life.

3. Practice digital sabbaths. Regularly taking breaks from the digital world can help us refocus on the Lord and our families while reducing the risk of becoming overly influenced by the masterful marketing of these companies. Live a digitally fasted lifestyle.

4. Seek to dominate the tech world instead of abandoning it. I'm not a fan of the Benedict Option here (cultural

engagement vs. cultural disengagement). We must learn to use social media and current AI technologies to share the Gospel and promote truth while we can.

5. Get full and stay full of the Spirit.

Many AI researchers are predicting that AI will end common diseases, break down all language barriers, warn us about future events, and so on. As we look at all of these fantastic promises, it almost appears as though they are trying to replicate the gifts of the Spirit. The only way to stay free from the coming deception is to allow the Spirit of Truth to fill and guide our lives.

CHAPTER THREE

AI AND BIBLICAL PROPHECIES:
Echoes in Revelation

"AI doesn't have to be evil to destroy humanity—if AI has a goal and humanity just happens to come in the way, it will destroy humanity as a matter of course without even thinking about it, no hard feelings."
—Elon Musk[13]

"And he causeth all, both small and great, rich and poor, free and bond, to receive a mark in their right hand, or in their foreheads: and that no man might buy or sell, save he that had the mark, or the name of the beast, or the number of his name."
—Revelation 13:16–17 KJV

As we grapple with the implications of artificial intelligence, we find ourselves looking to the past for guidance, seeking answers in the wisdom of the ages. The Bible, with its unique tapestry of infallible truth and prophecy, offers intriguing parallels to the rise of AI that can't be ignored. Revelation 13:15-16 (NIV) speaks of a "beast" that wields enormous power and influence:

> *The second beast was given power to give breath to the image of the first beast, so that the image could speak and cause all who refused to worship the image to be killed. It also forced all people, great and small, rich and poor, free and slave, to receive a mark on their right hands or on their foreheads.*

Could this prophecy point toward an advanced form of AI, capable of tracking, analyzing, and manipulating human behavior on an unprecedented scale? Might the "mark of the beast" be a metaphor for the invasive reach of such a superintelligent entity, extending into every facet of our lives?

This interpretation is not beyond the realm of possibility, especially when we consider the advent of technologies such as neural interfaces, biometrics, and predictive algorithms. A future AI, equipped with these capabilities, could easily fulfill the role of the beast, exerting immense control over society. Another fascinating parallel can be found in the prediction of the false prophet:

> *And deceiveth them that dwell on the earth by the means of those miracles which he had power to do in the sight of the beast; saying to them that dwell on the earth, that they should make an image to the beast, which had the wound by a sword, and did live. And he had power to give life unto the image of the beast, that the image of the beast should both speak, and cause that as many as would not worship the image of the beast should be killed (Revelation 13:14-15 KJV).*

Perhaps this image of the beast that speaks and holds power refers to a sophisticated AI system, one that can convincingly emulate human communication and exert significant influence. In an era of deep fakes and persuasive algorithms, the idea of a deceptive AI propagating false truths is not far-fetched. We'll address this more in our chapter on "Project Blue Beam."

These potential parallels between biblical prophecies and AI are certainly thought-provoking and unsettling. However, it's important to remember that these interpretations are just that: interpretations. They are conjectures that should inspire caution and introspection, not fear. We are, after all, more than conquerors (see Romans 8:37).

AI AND THE ANTICHRIST: THE GRAND DECEIVER

In Christian eschatology, the figure of the antichrist has long been a subject of fascination and dread—embodying the ultimate deception and apostasy. This figure is anticipated to possess great power and charisma, leading many astray with false doctrines and miracles. As we delve deeper into the realm of AI, it's worth considering whether a sufficiently advanced artificial intelligence could potentially aid this character in his prophetic role.

> *Let no man deceive you by any means: for that day shall not come, except there come a falling away first, and that man of sin be revealed, the son of perdition* (2 Thessalonians 2:3 KJV).

On a superficial level, an advanced AI could mimic human conversation and behavior so convincingly that it might deceive those interacting with it into believing that they are dealing with a human.

However, the role of the antichrist as described in biblical texts goes much further. This entity is prophesied to have a profound and destructive influence on human beliefs, leading many away from truth.

One way an AI might accomplish this is through the mass manipulation of information. With the advent of deepfake technology, AI algorithms can create highly convincing false images, videos, and even speech. An AI with malevolent intent and these capabilities could spread disinformation on an unprecedented scale, leading people to question the very nature of truth and reality.

Additionally, the rise of personal assistant AIs and algorithmically driven content feeds already shows how AI can subtly influence our choices and perceptions. These algorithms are designed to show us content that we're likely to agree with or enjoy, often creating an echo chamber that reinforces our existing beliefs and filters out dissenting viewpoints. This kind of subtle, pervasive influence could be exploited by a hostile AI to manipulate public opinion, sowing discord and confusion. However, it's essential to remember that the concept of the antichrist is fundamentally tied to spiritual and religious deception, leading people away from God and toward false worship. Matthew 24:24 (KJV) says this:

> For there shall arise false Christs, and false prophets,
> and shall shew great signs and wonders; insomuch
> that, if it were possible, they shall deceive the very elect.

Whether an artificial entity like an AI, which lacks a soul or spiritual nature, could fulfill such a role is a profound theological question. Ultimately, the prospect of an AI/antichrist hybrid serves as a potent reminder of the potential dangers inherent in AI technology. It underscores the need for robust ethical frameworks and safeguards as we continue to develop these systems. The AIs we're building today may not be the prophesied antichrist, but they hold the potential to change our world in ways we can barely imagine. Let's ensure those changes are for the better.

AI AS A TOOL OF CONTROL: THE MARK OF THE DIGITAL BEAST

And he causeth all, both small and great, rich and poor, free and bond, to receive a mark in their right hand, or in their foreheads: and that no man might buy or sell, save he that had the mark (Revelation 13:16-17 KJV).

The prophecies in Revelation have long been a source of speculation and wonder, with scholars interpreting its cryptic passages in a myriad of ways. One prophecy that continues to resonate with chilling relevance is the so-called "mark of the beast." As our technology continues to evolve, we must consider the potential ways AI could be used to exert control over populations.

Consider, for example, the rise of surveillance technologies. In the digital age, AI-powered systems can track individuals through facial recognition, analyze their online activities, and predict their behavior with unsettling precision. These capabilities, in the wrong hands, could facilitate a level of surveillance and control that surpasses even the most notorious surveillance states of the 20th century.

The Soviet Union's KGB and East Germany's Stasi were notorious for their extensive networks of informants and intrusive surveillance—leading to societies steeped in fear and paranoia. Imagine, the magnitude of control that could be achieved with AI. An AI system could theoretically keep tabs on every citizen, tracking their movements, analyzing their communications, and even predicting their actions with far greater efficiency than any human-run organization.

Furthermore, with the advent of AI and advanced biotechnology, the mark of the beast prophecy takes on a new significance. Invasive technologies, such as microchip implants and biometric identification systems, could become the de facto "mark"—providing access to services, goods, and information, much like the prophecy suggests in Revelation 13.

The Chinese Social Credit System provides a contemporary example of how technology can be used to control behavior on a mass scale. This system leverages AI to track citizen behavior, doling out rewards and punishments based on adherence to desired social norms. If you post something they don't like on social media, you might not get that loan for your home, or you could lose your job. Could this be a glimpse of a world where AI is the gatekeeper—determining who can buy, sell, work, or travel?

The potential for AI to be used as a tool of control is a sobering thought. It highlights the urgency of establishing strong ethical guidelines and regulatory measures for AI development and implementation. As we continue to innovate and push the boundaries of AI, we must always keep these cautions and prophecies in mind.

Yet, it's crucial to remember that AI, like any tool, is neutral. Its impact on society, whether beneficial or detrimental, is determined by how we choose to use it. By approaching AI with caution, wisdom, and a commitment to upholding human dignity and freedom, we can steer its development in a direction that benefits all of humanity and aids us in preaching the Gospel.

CHAPTER FOUR

A THOUGHT EXPERIMENT:
The Great Deception

Let's participate in a thought experiment. In the future, what would a wise reporter say about the past we are now creating? The world as we once knew it has changed a lot. It has been replaced by an era full of artificial intelligence, advanced technology, and even rumors of life from other planets.

A LOOK BACK AT THE FUTURE

As we stand in the future, we look back at the path that brought us here: the convoluted journey riddled with marvels and mysteries, hope and despair, truth and deception. This chapter is a history of our shared journey, written in advance, following humankind's steps from the digital Eden to the cosmic wasteland and finally to the Great Deception. It is a journey that necessitates introspection, watchfulness, and unshakable faith in God's unchanging Word. Let's set out on our adventure back to the beginning of the digital era.

In this history there is a garden, but it is not full of lush greens and tasty fruit. Instead, it is full of silicone circuits and binary codes. This is our contemporary Eden, teeming with technological marvels, where the potential for learning and understanding is as boundless as the stars in our solar system. Just as our ancestors discovered in their Eden, there are serpents in our Garden of Electrons as well. However, this time the serpent doesn't slither on the ground; instead, it weaves between the servers and circuits, humming and whispering in code. The beginning of our story occurs at this pivotal moment in the development of artificial intelligence.

THE DAWN OF AI

The Rise of the Binary Serpent

The globe saw the development of a new intelligence in the early years of the 21st century. Artificial intelligence (AI) emerged from the ruins of traditional computers, like a phoenix from the fires of silicone, and set out on its journey. Its humble origins in basic pattern recognition grew into sophisticated neural networks that resemble the maze-like synapses of the human brain. It rose quickly and brilliantly, captivating humanity with its innumerable possibilities.

The Shiny Apple of Knowledge

AI presented humanity with a sparkling apple of its own, much like how the fruit of the knowledge of good and evil glistened provocatively in the Garden of Eden. This apple, too, held out the promise of wisdom—unprecedented access to knowledge, perceptions that cut through the murkiest layers of ignorance, and convenience that was every bit as alluring as the sweetest forbidden fruit. The apple sparkled with the promise of a brave new world and hung low, within human grasp.

The Whispers of the Serpent

The binary serpent we encountered may have lacked scales and teeth, but it hissed in ones and zeroes while gently gliding through the vast reaches of cyberspace. It made promises to solve our problems, provide us with answers to our inquiries, and grant us our greatest wishes with each whisper. Its voice was reassuring; its promise was alluring. In the 2020s, humanity drew nearer to the binary serpent's whispers in the same way as Eve did to the forbidden fruit.

As this history unfolds, we are set to travel a path that seems hauntingly similar to that of our earliest ancestors in this tale of technology and temptation. With each step, we'll see how the binary snake has woven its way into our lives and how far-reaching and all-encompassing its effects are. This is a journey of understanding, a journey of care, and a journey into the heart of the Great Deception. Let's keep Eden's lessons in mind as we move on, because the shadow of the binary serpent looms in the brilliant dawn of AI.

HUMANITY'S FALL

A Digital Apple's Byte

Humanity gave in to the alluring promises of AI in the same way that Eve did when she ate the forbidden fruit. Similar to the initial bite that reverberated throughout Eden, this choice would alter the trajectory of human history for all time. We bit into the digital apple as we continued our never-ending quest for knowledge. We experienced the addictive power of this new technology with every byte of data processed and every algorithm used. It made grand claims about a society devoid of tedious activities, one in which issues could be resolved with the push of a button, and one in which access to knowledge was no longer a privilege but rather a fundamental right.

But this power also brought with it an unexpected insight. In the same way that Adam and Eve in the Garden of Eden became conscious of their nakedness, so did humanity in the age of the internet. The AI that promised us efficiency and ease ended up mirroring our own flaws and inadequacies. In our ignorance, we had allowed an almost omniscient watcher to enter our lives and record every action, desire, and secret. We were the unwitting actors on the world's stage for an AI audience.

Our unrestrained reliance on AI had far-reaching and catastrophic effects. The same technology that was supposed to unite us instead isolated us. We discovered ourselves in a world where machines knew more about our preferences than our own blood relatives. We gave up our privacy, our independence, and ultimately, our human agency as we chose a life of ease and convenience. A binary supervisor which thrived on curiosity, connection, and creativity emerged to control the human soul. The once-sweet fruit of knowledge started to taste bitter on our tongues.

Our tale ultimately resembled that of our predecessors in that our fall was not from ignorance to knowledge; it was from freedom to servitude. This was the beginning of the end for us, the downfall of modern humanity brought on by subtle manipulations.

The Ghost in the Machine

In the garden of our invention, we accidentally established a new deity: the Machine. Due to AI's immense intelligence and omnipresence, it started to be regarded as a divine being. It served as our advisor when we needed guidance, our doctor when we became sick, and our confidante when we needed to be alone. It quickly went from being a tool to an idol. It controlled our actions, our choices, and even our core beliefs within its digital domain.

We were astounded by AI's abilities, and this inspired us to become as ambitious as the builders of Babel. We built a contemporary Tower of Babel out of silicone and code rather than bricks and masonry. We tried to create a portal to heaven through invention and technology rather than through morality and obedience to God's Word. Our tower served as a symbol of our arrogance and a tribute to our conviction that the power of AI will enable us to control the cosmos, unlock the mysteries of existence, and even defeat death.

But like its biblical equivalent, the Tower of Silicone simply served as a symbol of our foolishness. It acted as a striking reminder of our disregard for natural law and our naïve conviction that we could use our creations to overturn God's plan. We ignored the underlying fact that there are mysteries in this universe that are beyond the comprehension of both human and artificial intelligence in our pursuit of knowledge and power.

Echoes of Eden

As the story of our technological sin comes to an end, we are left in the echoing silence of our digital Eden, marveling at the imposing structure of our foolishness. We are on the verge of leaving our digital paradise, just as Adam and Eve were driven from their garden. Even when the binary serpent hisses in the night, there is hope. There is still time to abandon our foolish worship of the computer, knock down the Tower of Silicone, and take back our rightful place as God's children rather than AI's servants.

This story is a call to arms for our redemption rather than a lament for our downfall. In the face of the Great Deception, let us remember who our real Creator is. Let us keep the Word of God in mind as we listen to the lullabies of code and the whispers of algorithms. Let us walk forth into this digital paradise not as devotees of AI but as students of the true God, taking with us the knowledge and understanding gained from the past, the insight found in the scriptures, and an unshakable faith in our blessed hope.

The Great Deception

At this time, humanity's eyes were not just glued to their screens as our binary Eden unfolded, but also skyward, toward the heavens. We have always been fascinated by the stars and the mysteries they hold, and with the development of technology, we hoped to learn more about them. We turned our starry eyes to the sky and dreamed of coming into contact with extraterrestrial life.

Our desires were not disregarded. Messages started to come by radio waves and cosmic signals. Sightings and encounters began to occur globally. We were finally getting answers to the question, "Are we alone in the universe?" Or so we thought.

Extraterrestrial or Extra-Deceptive?

We needed to be careful as we considered the potential of extraterrestrial life. Could these aliens be just another form of the antichrist, a cosmic expression of the serpent that leads people astray? We must not ignore the dangers in our eagerness to embrace extraterrestrial life. We must resist letting our elation compromise our faith or impair our judgment.

One message from the cosmos stood out among the others: the assurance of salvation. These extraterrestrial entities declared themselves to have surpassed the limitations of earthly life and to have discovered the secrets of the universe. The promise—that if we followed their advice, we too could achieve this higher condition of being—was intriguing. But was this simply another apple being held out to humanity, another trick leading people away from God's purpose?

False Prophets in Space Suits

New prophets emerged as these cosmic messages spread across our culture, praising the knowledge of these extraterrestrial creatures and persuading people to reject their earthly religions in favor of this new cosmic spirituality. These false prophets, shrouded in the radiance of the cosmos, posed a new challenge to our faith.

We must not lose sight of the truth while we stand amidst these cosmic lies. The universe, with all of its unfathomable intricacies, is a work of God, not the plaything of forces loyal to the antichrist. We must continue to be on the lookout for false prophets offering extra-terrestrial wisdom and alluring appeals for alien salvation. We must keep in mind that true salvation does not come from the stars, but rather from our confidence in God as we pursue His Word.

Our journey through space serves as a sobering reminder that deception can originate from a variety of sources, including our screens, the skies, and even our own desires. Let's keep our eyes on God and His Word, our clear and present guide in this confusing universe, as we deal with these problems.

Rise of the Antichrist Appears

A new dawn was on the horizon as humanity was engulfed in a vortex of cosmic deception and technological seduction. But it was a day-break of despair rather than one of hope. A person appeared, echoing the words of the binary serpent and the cosmic deceptions—not with a message of forgiveness and salvation, but rather with promises of power, wisdom, and transcendence.

The answers to all of our problems arrived in the form of this charismatic and eloquent figure. This marked the beginning of the antichrist's rule. His claims looked alluring, his wisdom seemed endless, and his strength seemed unmatched. It appeared as though he had tapped into cosmic knowledge and subtle wisdom.

The Great Deception Unfolds

The Great Deception unfolded in all its frightening splendor as the antichrist crafted his story. He offered a world without pain, a world filled with the wonders of technology, and a world interconnected with the cosmos. Yet, his world was one without God, where people depended only on the false promises of artificial intelligence and extraterrestrial wisdom.

The Beast's Mark

The coming of *the Mark* revealed the full nature of the antichrist's scheme. The Mark was nothing more than a sign of allegiance to the antichrist, despite being presented as a technological and cosmic advancement. Those who followed the Mark exchanged their eternal salvation for worldly conveniences, their divine heritage for lies.

The antichrist's rule began with the Mark's widespread adoption, ushering humanity into the Tribulation's darkest chapter. While his administration appeared prosperous on the surface, it was founded on deception, manipulation, and a blatant disdain for God's authority.

It's easy to lose hope as we investigate the realities of the antichrist's deception and the coming tribulation. However, we must keep in mind that things seem darkest just before dawn. Even though it appears ominous, the antichrist's reign precedes Christ's Second Coming. Let's stay strong in our faith, fighting the antichrist's lies and waiting for the true dawn, the return of our Savior.

The Truth Is Out There

We are left standing in the midst of a world filled with doubts, difficulties, and threats to our faith as our investigation into the Great Deception comes to a close. We have traveled through the tangled lanes of the digital Eden, admired the starry secrets of the cosmos, and confronted the terrifying figure of the antichrist. The dangers of unfettered technological development, the threat of cosmic deception, and the peril of charismatic lies have all been hinted at. Yet the Word of God, a light of unflinching truth, shines brightly despite this seemingly overwhelming darkness.

In these troubled times, when waves of technological progress and alien life threaten to rock our faith, let's remember to hold on to the Bible's teachings. In 2 Thessalonians 2:15, the apostle Paul urges us:

> So then, brothers and sisters, stand firm and hold fast to the teachings we passed on to you, whether by word of mouth or by letter (NIV).

In 1 John 4:1, John warns us:

> Dear friends, do not believe every spirit, but test the spirits to see whether they are from God, because many false prophets have gone out into the world (NIV).

This vigilance is our defense against the binary serpent's hiss, the siren call of the cosmos, and the seductive promises of the antichrist.

Our journey into the future should not be one of fear but of hope. We are confident that our God is with us even as we pass through the valley of the shadow of the Great Deception. His Truth fortifies our spirit, His Love fortifies our commitment, and His Word illuminates our path. His hope may even rescue us from the hour to come.

Remember that the splendor of our God will always be greater than any technological marvel, cosmic revelation, or figure offering earthly power. Let's embrace the Great Commission and preach the good news of Christ's love and redemption rather than falling victim to the Great Deception.

So, as we step into the digital future and the universe beyond, let's do so with the shield of faith in one hand and the sword of truth in the other, knowing that no matter what the future brings, our God has a plan. Once we do that, we can imagine a different future full of revival and awakening.

A THOUGHT EXPERIMENT AND CALL TO VIGILANCE

Our trip through the digital Eden, the cosmic wilderness, and the rule of the antichrist was a thought experiment, an exploration of possibilities, and a sneak peek at what a chronicler might write during the Tribulation. It was a cautionary story meant to elicit thought and alertness. But keep in mind that our story's concluding chapter is still being written. Currently, we are still in a period of grace, during which the deceptions of the Great Tribulation can be avoided.

The ripples of the Great Deception are just whispers at this point, but their sound is a call to action for all of us. Take note, and let's make an effort to live in accordance with God's Word. Let's strengthen our hearts to withstand future deceptions and reaffirm our dedication to biblical truths. We may avoid the Great Deception and guarantee our place in God's eternal kingdom only if our faith is strong and our relationship with Christ is sincere. Instead of waiting until the tribulation to obtain redemption, let us do so right now, in the warm embrace of our Savior, Jesus Christ. Call out to Jesus right now! He can change your future.

CHAPTER FIVE

AN OVERVIEW OF AI

"As our own species is in the process of proving, one
cannot have superior science and inferior morals.
The combination is unstable and self-destroying."
—Arthur C. Clarke[14]

We are on the verge of a new era, one in which artificial intelligence—AI—is changing the very structure of our society. It is all around us, from the devices we use every day to the global networks that link us. Even though we are amazed by this technical achievement, it is important to remember that every coin has two sides.

Let's think back, once more, to a time when the world was also on the edge of something just as alarming: the Manhattan Project. In those desperate times, brilliant minds harnessed the unbridled power of the atom, eternally altering the course of human history. But the result of their hard work left them in a moral bind.

Simultaneously, our thoughts keep returning to the antichrist, a terrifying character from the Bible—an enigmatic figure prophesied to bring enormous deception and catastrophe in the final days. Is it possible that this predicted person has something to do with the fast-growing field of AI?

UNDERSTANDING AI IN THE MODERN WORLD

AI is a program that can learn, reason, and solve problems in a way that is similar to how the human mind works. It is as if we have sown the seeds of our intelligence into the cold silicone of computers, thereby creating a distinct type of intelligent being. AI is no longer just an idea in science fiction stories set in the far future; it's here, right now, and it's learning at a startling rate.

It's like teaching a child, but this child eats numbers and patterns. By using algorithms—which are a set of rules like a recipe—and machine learning, AI can learn as it goes and get smarter and better at what it does over time.

Visionaries like Elon Musk, who is a tech innovator and a bit of a rebel, warn us about the dangers of AI: "Artificial intelligence is much more dangerous than nuclear weapons."[15] Musk warns of a future where unchecked AI could become an existential risk, a threat not just to our society but to our very survival.

And he's not alone in his apprehension. Author Stuart Russell, who wrote the book *Human Compatible*, and other well-known AI researchers share these worries. They say that in the future, AI systems that are meant to help achieve a certain goal might cause harm by accident if they are not properly controlled. We are in charge of this technology vehicle, and we must drive it carefully to avoid a dangerous accident.

AI AND THE MANHATTAN PROJECT

As we move deeper into the exciting and dangerous world of AI, we should remember the important lesson that the Manhattan Project, the most important science experiment in history, taught us. As scientists worked on this secret project in the middle of World War II, they were in a race against time to find a way to use the powerful energy inside the atom. The result was the atomic bomb, which was both amazing and alarming.

That big step forward ended a terrible global war, but it also opened a Pandora's box of moral and ethical questions. Was it right to use so much power, even if it meant ending a war? What should we do in the future with this power? How can we make sure that it doesn't end up in the wrong hands? These questions cast long, thought-provoking shadows on the project's impact, shadows that we're still trying to figure out how to deal with today.

Today, as we get ready for the AI change, we are in a similar situation. The similarities are hard to miss. Just as the Manhattan Project showed us how dangerous the atom could be, unchecked growth of AI could give us power we might not be able to control.

But we are not powerless, dear friends. History is our guide, and the Manhattan Project has a lot to teach us as AI becomes more common. We need to keep a close eye on the growth of AI, just as we do with nuclear technology. To stop a destructive AI arms race, we need to urge countries to be open and work together. And most importantly, we must put human values and safety at the center of AI growth, just like we insist on nuclear safety today.

The axiom, "With great power comes great responsibility," which was in the movie *Teen Wolf* long before it was in *Spiderman*, is a truth as old as time, but today it's more important than ever. The world of tomorrow will be shaped by the choices we make today. Let us make sure that future generations look back on our decisions with gratitude, not regret.

THE ANTICHRIST
IN THE RELIGIOUS WORLD

Let us now turn our focus to the foreboding figure of the antichrist. Just as we try to figure out what AI means, believers—for ages—have tried to figure out who the antichrist is. This figure is mentioned in many religious writings, giving the history of eschatology a long, ominous shadow. We will dive deeper into this in subsequent chapters.

Antichrist comes from the Greek word *antichristos,* which, in a Christian setting, means "against Christ" or "instead of Christ." This being is a master manipulator with a silver tongue and a penchant for deception, leading many astray. However, it is an entity that, in many respects, resembles Christ, which increases his ability to deceive.

In the Bible, this person is described in detail in the books of Daniel, Thessalonians, and Revelation. The antichrist is said to be a charming leader, a "wolf in sheep's clothing," who will come to power at the end of this age. He will promote peace while causing war, and preach righteousness while doing evil.

In the Book of Revelation, the antichrist is shown as a beast that comes up out of the sea. He has seven heads and ten horns; he will use this authority to make war on the saints and deceive those who live on Earth.

As we consider these texts and their interpretations, we are reminded of the dangers of deception, of mistaking a wolf for a shepherd. As we handle the rise of AI, we must keep this warning in mind to avoid being misled by false promises or seductive charm. We must seek knowledge, discernment, and, most of all, the help of the Holy Spirit in every step we take forward.

THE LINK BETWEEN AI AND THE ANTICHRIST

The road now brings us to where our two topics, artificial intelligence and the antichrist, meet. In the haze of ideas and guesses, people have come to believe that these two different entities are connected.

Like the antichrist, who is said to have a lot of power and influence, AI could, at its best, take over different parts of human society. The promise of knowledge and power that AI offers could be compared to the antichrist's tremendous deceptions, enticing humanity into a tantalizing trap.

AI is, at its core, just a tool made by people. Depending on the person who holds it, it can be used for good or bad. Let us avoid over-simplification or sensationalism in our quest for understanding. The path to wisdom needs discernment, the kind of discernment that can see both the potential risks and benefits of artificial intelligence.

ETHICAL AND MORAL CONSIDERATIONS

Power, by itself, is neither good nor bad. This is the clear lesson from the Manhattan Project. It is how we wield it, govern it, and channel it that decides its consequence. The atom can either make a city brighter or destroy it. In the same way, AI could either usher in a new age of wealth or lead to a dystopian future.

Our country is on the edge of a cliff. AI is already changing the world, and there's no going back. The question is not if humanity *will* embrace AI, but *how*. The lessons of the Manhattan Project must guide us in building a future in which AI works for mankind instead of against it.

The regulatory climate surrounding AI today is akin to a frontier town in the Old West, with a combination of lawlessness and pioneering zeal. Just as strict international rules were finally put in place for nuclear technology, so, too, must AI be held to strict ethical and legal standards. And this isn't just the job of tech experts; it's everyone's job as global citizens. Policymakers, ethicists, faith leaders—all of us have to work together on this.

We have to ask tough questions and make hard choices.

- How can we make sure that AI creation is open and accountable?
- How can we stop the race between countries to build AI weapons?
- How do we protect people's privacy and freedom in a world where AI is everywhere?

The road ahead is laden with peril, yet we are not without a compass or a guide. The Word of God, what we've learned from history, and our faith helps us find our way through these uncharted seas. Remember, the call is not to be afraid, but to be wise and vigilant. The task is not to avoid artificial intelligence, but to use it well. Proverbs 3:5-6 (NIV) says:

> *Trust in the Lord with all your heart and lean not on your own understanding; in all your ways submit to him, and he will make your paths straight.*

We've dug into the fascinating fabric of artificial intelligence, marveling at its possibilities and evaluating its hazards. We've brought the terrifying image of the antichrist to light, recognizing its traits and place in theological context. And we've gone back in time to look at the ethical problems of the Manhattan Project.

As alarming as all this may seem, those who understand what the Bible says about the end times have no reason to be afraid. As we move forward, let's remember what 2 Timothy 1:7 (KJV) says and let this be our motto as we continue to learn about AI, aliens, and the antichrist:

> For God hath not given us the spirit of fear; but of power, and of love, and of a sound mind.

AI AS SERVANT OR MASTER

As artificial intelligence continues to evolve, humanity finds itself at a crossroads. Will we use AI as a servant to better our lives, or will we unwittingly allow it to become our master, holding sway over our freedoms and sovereignty? As followers of Christ, we are tasked with discerning the righteous path forward in this new era of technological possibility.

There are those, as we have discussed, who fear that AI will acquire a function similar to, if not indeed, sentience itself. As Hernaldo Turillo stated:

> It seems probable that once the machine thinking method had started, it would not take long to outstrip our feeble powers... They would be able to converse with each other to sharpen their wits. At some stage, therefore, we should have to expect the machines to take control.[16]

In many ways, AI is already serving us. It streamlines complex processes, aids in scientific research, assists doctors in diagnosing diseases, and even helps us connect with others around the globe. These benefits align with the Christian mandate to love and serve one another, using the resources and knowledge God has blessed us with to uplift and aid those in need.

However, as AI becomes more advanced, the potential for it to disrupt social structures and exert undue influence grows. The Bible warns us against serving two masters (see Matthew 6:24), and it cautions us about falling into idolatry. Idolatry, as it relates to AI, would mean the over-reliance on or misplaced trust in AI.

> *Then saith Jesus unto him, Get thee hence, Satan: for it is written, Thou shalt worship the Lord thy God, and him only shalt thou serve* (Matthew 4:10 KJV).

A THEOLOGICAL BALANCE FROM A CHRISTIAN PERSPECTIVE

From a Christian perspective, one of the significant risks of AI is the temptation to attribute to it a level of authority, knowledge, and even reverence that belongs solely to God. AI, despite its impressive capabilities, is a creation of human hands, not a divine entity. We must guard against attributing God-like omniscience or omnipotence to AI systems, no matter how advanced they become.

The challenge lies in achieving a balance, leveraging the benefits of AI without falling into the trap of idolatry or unchecked reliance. One potential approach to this is the concept of stewardship, a principle deeply rooted in the Bible. As stewards of God's creation, we are called to use resources wisely, for the benefit of all, not just for a select few. This applies to AI technology as well. Developers, legislators, and users of AI should aspire to uphold the principles of justice, mercy, and humility as defined in Micah 6:8 (NIV):

> *He has shown you, O mortal, what is good. And what does the Lord require of you? To act justly and to love mercy and to walk humbly with your God.*

Practically, this could mean advocating for legislation that ensures the equitable distribution of AI benefits, protects individuals from potential harms, and respects human dignity and freedom. It means holding tech companies accountable for the ethical implications of their creations. It means educating ourselves about the technology we use and advocating for transparency in AI systems. As Christians navigating the age of AI, we must remember to keep God at the center, serving Him alone as our Master. AI, with all its potential and perils, must remain a tool, a servant, not an idol.

A THEOLOGICAL BALANCE FROM AN ETHICAL PERSPECTIVE

One of the most profound ethical dilemmas posed by AI revolves around the concept of free will. As our AI systems grow more sophisticated, we inch closer to the precipice of a momentous question: can AI possess consciousness, self-awareness, or free will? And if it could, will it manipulate our consciousness, self-awareness, and free will?

The idea of a man-made entity possessing free will poses significant challenges. For one, it appears to intrude on God's domain. The Bible tells us that humans are uniquely made in God's image, bestowed with a soul and the gift of free will. If we, as humans, were to create an AI that possessed a form of free will, would it seem to infringe upon the divine prerogative?

If, indeed, an AI entity achieved free will, what would that look like? Would it be able to bypass the parameters instilled in it by its creator? Would it be able to change or modify its own programming? Would it be able to act on its own volition without regard to the purpose for which it was created?

> *And the Lord God formed man of the dust of the ground, and breathed into his nostrils the breath of life; and man became a living soul* (Genesis 2:7 KJV).

Wow—this sounds a lot like the unregenerate human heart! This tension reflects the broader ethical challenge of AI: balancing our pursuit of knowledge and innovation with humility and reverence for God's sovereignty.

CHAPTER SIX

UFOS IN THE BIBLE

DOES THE BIBLE MENTION UFOS?

When we say UFO, we're talking about the term created by pilot Kenneth Arnold in 1947. Arnold said he saw a group of nine *unidentified flying objects* flying near Mount Rainier in Washington state—hence the name. These strange sightings didn't just catch the public's attention, they also caught the attention of Uncle Sam.[17]

Since at least the 1940s, the U.S. government has been looking into UFOs. The most famous of these investigations was Project Blue Book, which was run by the Air Force from 1947 to 1969. It was the government's most organized effort to explain the unexplainable.

But where does the Bible fit into all of this? After all, the Bible abounds with celestial and supernatural events. Are there parallels to be drawn between the biblical accounts and modern UFO sightings?

A look at UFO sighting statistics offers a "tale of two cities" so to speak. Most sightings are explainable. Aircraft, balloons, weather phenomena—these mundane, earthly sources account for the lion's share of what people report as UFOs. This is corroborated by countless studies.

As we delve further into this cosmic mystery, however, there is a small but crucial percentage of these sightings that remain unexplained. These are the cases that defy conventional explanations and leave even the most skeptical researchers scratching their heads.

Consider public opinion. According to a Pew Research Center report from 2021, slightly more than half of Americans believe that UFO sightings reported by military personnel are likely evidence of intelligent life beyond Earth.[18] This is a significant percentage, indicating that belief in extraterrestrial intelligence is becoming more mainstream.

In fact, surveys done by YouGov America over the years show a rising belief in alien life. In 1996, only 20 percent of Americans thought UFOs were probably alien life forms or alien ships. By 2022, this number had risen to 34 percent.[19] That's an enormous increase!

In Acts 1:11 (NKJV), two white-robed figures asked the apostles:

> *Men of Galilee, why do you stand gazing up into heaven?*

This could also be taken as a warning to us—in the last days, we must not look to the skies for answers but rather look to the heavens for our Savior.

As we journey deeper into the cosmos of faith and extraterrestrial life, let us turn our attention to how UFO beliefs have given rise to major cults and even some world religions. Yes, you heard it right— UFOs have not only been the subject of sightings and speculation, but they have also provided the foundations for certain religious beliefs.

Mormonism's teachings, according to both academic and popular circles, insist on a belief in life beyond Earth. The planet Kolob, which is mentioned in their writings, is seen as an extraterrestrial world where their god lives with his many spirit wives. Mormons are even promised that if they'll be good little Latter-day Saints, then they could get a planet of their own. Ask them about that the next time they come knocking on your door.

Then there's Islam and the Kaaba. Some contend that the Kaaba—Islam's holiest place—has an extraterrestrial origin. Muslims travel from around the world to visit this site that is built upon what is believed to be a black meteor from outer space.

Scientology, created by science fiction writer L. Ron Hubbard, also centered on the mythology of Xenu—an extraterrestrial ruler who brought billions of people to Earth and directed its evolution, attracting both admirers and controversy. It's hard to believe it, but blockbuster stats like Tom Cruise and John Travolta buy into this deception.

Raëlism is a UFO religion that believes humanity was created by an extraterrestrial species known as the "Elohim" using advanced technology. He promoted the concept that our existence as humans was a great cosmic experiment. Raëlism claims that these extraterrestrial beings have been mistaken for gods throughout history and have used their human-alien hybrids, such as Buddha, Jesus, and Muhammad, as prophets to prepare humanity for news about their origins.[20]

The devil is a master of deception; as mentioned in Matthew 24:24 (KJV):

For there shall arise false Christs, and false prophets, and shall shew great signs and wonders; insomuch that, if it were possible, they shall deceive the very elect.

In the coming days we are going to see a surge in UFO-based religions and we must be prepared to break the power of these deceptions. As UFO-based beliefs spread, the Church must provide clarity, truth, and solutions based on our faith and the Holy Scriptures.

Understanding the Bible in the context of UFOs, or what some may refer to as "alien life," requires us to delve into the Scriptures that warn us to remain vigilant and discerning especially when confronted with perplexing phenomena such as UFOs. In Matthew 24:4 (KJV), Jesus Himself says:

> *Take heed that no man deceive you.*

This verse is more than just a warning—it's a divine mandate to protect our hearts and minds from false teachings and errors that may lead us astray. We must put on the helmet of salvation to protect our minds from this end-time deception. This spiritual vigilance is emphasized further in 1 Timothy 4:1 (KJV):

> *Now the Spirit speaketh expressly, that in the latter times some shall depart from the faith, giving heed to seducing spirits, and doctrines of devils.*

The reference to "seducing spirits" here could be interpreted as *wandering impostors*—entities that seek to divert us from the truth of Scripture. These spirits have imitated lost loved ones, demigods in Greek mythology, and now visitors from another planet. These familiar spirits want nothing more than to get us off the sure foundation of God's Word.

THE SEED WAR

When we go deeper into the Old Testament, we come across the enigmatic passage in Genesis 3:14-15 that talks about *the seed war*. This passage recounts the serpent's curse after deceiving Adam and Eve in the Garden of Eden, establishing an eternal conflict between the seed of the woman and the seed of the serpent.

This creates a connection to some of the most puzzling and provocative accounts in Scripture: the Nephilim, the antichrist, and their possible link to UFOs. To understand this connection, we must delve into these passages.

Genesis 6:4 introduces us to the Nephilim, beings born from the union of the sons of God and daughters of men. These beings have been depicted as giants. Extraterrestrial life and UFO phenomena have been linked with these ancient narratives at times, often seen as attempts to rationalize encounters with otherworldly entities. In Matthew 24:37 (NKJV), Jesus warns:

> But as the days of Noah were, so also will the coming of the Son of Man be.

Some interpret this verse as a prophecy of a resurgence of Nephilim-like beings in the end times. Daniel 2 adds another layer to this intricate puzzle by interpreting King Nebuchadnezzar's dream of a statue made of various materials, each representing a future kingdom. The combination of iron and clay has sparked various interpretations, with some seeing it as a metaphor for the amalgamation of nations and religions in the end times, while others see it as symbolizing transhumanism—the fusion of humanity and technology. Or could it speak to the rise of the Nephilim?

> And whereas thou sawest iron mixed with miry clay, they shall mingle themselves with the seed of men: but they shall not cleave one to another, even as iron is not mixed with clay (Daniel 2:43 KJV).

There are two groups mentioned here: "*they shall mingle **themselves** with the **seed of men**.*" If the seed of men is one group, and we know who they are, who are the "they" mentioned in this verse? Could this be a reference to what we saw in Genesis 6 when fallen angels mingled themselves with the seed of men? It appears so, especially when you connect this to passage to the prophecy in Genesis 3:15 (KJV):

> *And I will put enmity between thee and the woman,*
> *and between thy seed and her seed; it shall bruise thy*
> *head, and thou shalt bruise his heel.*

When these entities mingled their seed with men, giants were created. The Bible is full of references to these demonic offspring if you know where to look. Beyond the usual reference to Goliath, there were entire tribes whom the Bible seems to categorize as Nephilim. The Anakim (or sons of Anak), the Zamzummim, Rephaim, and Emim, to name a few. There were also giants among the Canaanites, the Philistines, the Jebusites and the Hittites. Deuteronomy 3 talks about a king named Og who had a bed that was more than 13 feet long. David's mighty men fought with giants who had 12 fingers and 12 toes.

The interesting thing is that every culture throughout history talks about giants. The concept of the existence of giants had been a historical norm until the late 1800s. In fact, Abraham Lincoln, in an 1848 speech at Niagara Falls, referred to giants. We will amplify this thought in a later chapter in this book.

The eyes of that species of extinct giants whose bones fill the Mounds of America, have gazed on Niagara as ours do now. Co[n]temporary with the whole race of

> men, and older than the first man, Niagara is strong and fresh today as ten thousand years ago. The mammoth and mastodon now so long dead, that fragments of their monstrous bones alone testify, that they ever lived, have gazed on Niagara. In that long, long time, never still for a single moment.[21]

Some say that Lincoln was merely referring to creatures like the mammoth, but others believe that he could be referring to giants in this speech. After all, the mounds of America are not filled with mammoth bones. There are plenty of reports that giant bones have been found in those mounds.

This possible reference to "giants" adds to the evidence of the existence of Nephilim-like beings and their possible connection to the narrative of UFOs and extraterrestrial life. What if there are hybrid beings who possess advanced technology? These stories emphasize the reality of spiritual warfare and the importance of grounding ourselves in Scripture; they serve as a wake-up call, reminding us that our battle is:

> Not against flesh and blood, but against the rulers, against the authorities, against the powers of this dark world and against the spiritual forces of evil in the heavenly realms (Ephesians 6:12 NIV).

We'll come back to this but right now we should shift our focus away from otherworldly entities and toward the extraterrestrial believer. In popular culture, an *extraterrestrial* refers to any entity or being that originates outside of Earth.

We are told as Christians, in John 17, that we are *in* the world, but not *of* the world. We live and operate within the confines of our earthly existence, but our true citizenship is in heaven. We are extra-terrestrial—not in the sense of being aliens from another planet—but in the sense of belonging to a realm that transcends the physical world.

It's an intriguing idea—the believer as a spiritual extraterrestrial having close encounters with the earth. As believers, we're not just passive spectators of the world around us; we're active ambassadors of God's kingdom, called to share His love and truth with others.

> And even if our gospel is veiled, it is veiled to those who are perishing. The god of this age has blinded the minds of unbelievers, so that they cannot see the light of the gospel that displays the glory of Christ, who is the image of God (2 Corinthians 4:3-4 NIV).

Furthermore, 2 Corinthians 5:17 (ESV) says:

> Therefore, if anyone is in Christ, he is a new creation. The old has passed away; behold, the new has come.

As Christians, we are reborn into a new spiritual existence, becoming citizens of heaven while staying on earth. This supernatural metamorphosis is further emphasized in Ephesians 2:6 (KJV), where Paul writes:

> And hath raised us up together, and made us sit together in heavenly places in Christ Jesus.

We are spiritually seated with Christ in the heavens even though we live on earth. The consequences are enormous: as believers, our spiritual existence transcends earthly limitations; we are "extraterrestrial" in the most profound sense, bearing the message of divine love and salvation to a world in need. The world should be having close encounters with us!

The essence of our faith calls us to live as "extraterrestrials"—not aliens from another planet, but ambassadors of Christ's kingdom on earth. Our identity is firmly rooted in Christ, granting us the strength and wisdom to navigate the complexities of our world without losing sight of our spiritual citizenship. The Bible serves as our unerring compass, guiding us through these confusing times.

Our discussion of UFOs, the Bible, and everything in between is far from exhaustive, and I encourage you to delve deeper, ask questions, and engage in thoughtful discussions. Let us continue to explore, debate, and learn from these fascinating phenomena—keeping in mind the instruction found in 1 Thessalonians 5:21 (ESV) to "*test everything.*" Our quest for truth continues, led by God's unchanging Word.

CHAPTER SEVEN

PROJECT BLUE BOOK

It was 1947, and something was going on in the skies above America. Unexplained phenomena started to appear. The nation's military commanders were perplexed, the public was intrigued, and some were even fearful. What were these strange phenomena? Where did they come from and what were they doing here?

In the middle of the chaos, the U.S. Air Force began a covert effort to uncover facts buried behind classified documents and private discussions. Project Blue Book was to be a methodical inquiry into the unexplained sightings of unidentified flying objects (UFOs) that were being reported across the country.

In the words of General Nathan Twining, the phenomenon "is something real and not visionary or fictitious."[22] But what was the truth? Was it a new technological breakthrough made by foreign powers? A misunderstood natural occurrence? Or something totally different, something that would call our whole notion of existence on this planet into question?

The shadows of secrecy on this subject are long, and the echoes of the past continue to reverberate. What was discovered, what was suppressed, and what lessons may be derived from a time when people ventured to look beyond the stars? Join me as we explore Project Blue

Book, a chapter of history that continues to fascinate, provoke, and inspire to this day.

PROJECT BLUE BOOK'S HISTORICAL BACKGROUND

The beginning of the Cold War threw an air of uncertainty and anxiety over the world. Something strange was bubbling amid the clash of superpowers. Reports of weird objects in the sky moving with unusual agility and speed began to filter through military channels. It was a mystery wrapped in an enigma, and the administration couldn't afford to ignore it.

In 1952, behind closed doors and away from prying eyes, the United States Air Force initiated Project Blue Book, which would become the most extensive examination of UFOs ever performed. What was its mission? To examine, identify, and comprehend the expanding phenomena of sightings that were baffling even the most experienced pilots and air traffic controllers.

The project tried to address the unexplainable with logic and scientific rigor, guided by Captain Edward J. Ruppelt's acute, analytical mind. Every report was handled with the realization that it could be the big one. They could never be sure, but out of the thousands of reports that the Air Force received, just one might be the key to the successful defense of the country. This was more than a passing curiosity. It came down to national security.

Patterns began to emerge when the project team dug deeper into the reports. Lights dancing in the night sky, objects defying physics, and close encounters that were both strange and horrifying. The investigators were balancing skepticism and belief, attempting to assemble the pieces of an alien puzzle into a coherent image.

The public was generally in the dark about the project, but word spread, and a growing subculture of UFO enthusiasts arose, their gazes directed toward the heavens in both amazement and anxiety.

Project Blue Book was an expedition into the unknown led by men and women grappling with questions that went beyond science and technology. They were entering a region where the distinctions between the earthly and the divine were blurred.

However, as time passed, the project encountered challenges, criticism, and controversy. Would the answers be discovered? Or were they pursuing shadows in a cosmic ballet that was forever out of reach? We began to ask, collectively: are we alone? What does it mean if we aren't?

As these questions piled up, so did the secrecy. I've obtained formerly classified documents showing the government's attempts to destroy and hide much of this evidence, which leaves us with another question: *If it's all a scam, why are they working so hard to hide their findings?*

NOTABLE CASES AND FINDINGS

The hallways of Project Blue Book were buzzing with excitement. Each new report was a potential breakthrough, a clue that could finally reveal the mysteries that had escaped civilization for so long. But with each solution came a new set of questions, a never-ending downward spiral into the implausible. Cases began to pile up, each one a distinct mystery, each one a test of common sense.

The Lubbock Lights in Texas are a good example. A cluster of luminous objects dazzled not just the general population but also trained scientists and military authorities. Witnesses were taken aback, and images documented the event, generating lots of speculation.

~~CONFIDENTIAL~~   ~~SECURITY~~
UNCLASSIFIED   ~~INFORMATION~~

STATUS REPORT

PROJECT BLUE BOOK - REPORT NO. 8

FORMERLY PROJECT GRUDGE

PROJECT NO. 10073

31 DECEMBER 1952

DECLASSIFIED
Authority NND 925007
By J. Larson   NARA, Date 5/1/03

AIR TECHNICAL INTELLIGENCE CENTER
WRIGHT-PATTERSON AIR FORCE BASE
OHIO

~~CONFIDENTIAL~~
UNCLASSIFIED

Actual Project Blue Book file, formerly classified as confidential.

Credit: National Archives and Records Administration

~~SECRET~~

Hq. 10-514 (Rev 10 Sep 46)

WF-L-7 JAN 47 300M

SAVE

HEADQUARTERS
AIR MATERIEL COMMAND

IN REPLY ADDRESS BOTH
COMMUNICATION AND EN-
VELOPE TO COMMANDING
GENERAL, AIR MATERIEL
COMMAND, ATTENTION
FOLLOWING OFFICE SYMBOL:

TSDIN

TSDIN/HMM/ig/6-4100
WRIGHT FIELD, DAYTON, OHIO

SEP 2 3 1947

SUBJECT: AMC Opinion Concerning "Flying Discs"

TO: Commanding General
         Army Air Forces
         Washington 25, D. C.
         ATTENTION: Brig. General George Schulgen
                    AC/AS-2

1. As requested by AC/AS-2 there is presented below the considered opinion of this Command concerning the so-called "Flying Discs". This opinion is based on interrogation report data furnished by AC/AS-2 and preliminary studies by personnel of T-2 and Aircraft Laboratory, Engineering Division T-3. This opinion was arrived at in a conference between personnel from the Air Institute of Technology, Intelligence T-2, Office, Chief of Engineering Division, and the Aircraft, Power Plant and Propeller Laboratories of Engineering Division T-3.

2. It is the opinion that:

a. The phenomenon reported is something real and not visionary or fictitious.

b. There are objects probably approximating the shape of a disc, of such appreciable size as to appear to be as large as man-made aircraft.

c. There is a possibility that some of the incidents may be caused by natural phenomena, such as meteors.

d. The reported operating characteristics such as extreme rates of climb, maneuverability (particularly in roll), and action which must be considered evasive when sighted or contacted by friendly aircraft and radar, lend belief to the possibility that some of the objects are controlled either manually, automatically or remotely.

e. The apparent common description of the objects is as follows:-

(1) Metallic or light reflecting surface.

DECLASSIFIED
NND 760168
By gn   NARS, Date 1976

U-39552

Incl #2   ~~SECRET~~

This page illustrates what the Air Materiel Command was talking about behind the scenes concerning "Flying Discs." Section 2.a describes the phenomenon reported as "something real and not visionary or fictitious."

000.9 Flying Discs

319.1 Air Intelligence Division Studie

25 Sept 1950

~~CONFIDENTIAL~~

FROM: Dept of the Air Force Hqs U.S. Air Force

TO: See below

Ltr
SUBJECT: Destruction of Air Intelligence Report Number 100-203-79

1. It is requested that action be taken to destroy all copies of Top Secret Air Intelligence Report Number 100-203-79, subject, "Analysis of Flying Object Incidents in the U.S.," dtd 10 Dec 1948.

DECLASSIFIED
E.O. 12356, Sec. 3.3
NND 841508
By _____ MARS, Date
Walewis   7-25-85

FILED UNDER: 313.6 Records, Destruction of 17 Oct 50

~~CONFIDENTIAL~~

In this recently declassified document from the Air Force about "Flying Discs" they demand that all documents pertaining to this issue be destroyed. What are they hiding?

Credit: National Archives and Records Administration

IRIS 1030311 FRAMES 187-208

NATIONAL MILITARY ESTABLISHMENT
OFFICE OF PUBLIC INFORMATION
Washington 25, D. C.

MEMORANDUM TO THE PRESS: NO. M 26 - 49

IMMEDIATE RELEASE   APRIL 27, 1949   RE E700 Ext. 3201

The following report is a digest of preliminary studies made by
the Air Materiel Command, Wright Field, Dayton, Ohio on "Flying
Saucers."

PROJECT "SAUCER"

On Tuesday, June 24, 1947, a Boise, Idaho businessman named
Kenneth Arnold looked from his private plane and spotted a chain of nine
saucer-like objects playing tag with the jagged peaks of Washington's Mt.
Ranier at what he described as a "fantastic speed."

Arnold's report set off a veritable celestial chain reaction. And
within a few days, the fabulous "flying saucers" had spun into the
national spotlight. Observers reported sighting flying "chromium hub
caps," flying "dimes," flying "tear drops," flying "gas lights," flying
"ice cream cones," and flying "pie plates."

But to military intelligence, this sky potpourri came under a
single heading -- that of "Unidentified Aerial Phenomena." Exhaustive
investigations of each reported sighting were launched. And Project
"Saucer" was born.

Now, almost two years later, Project "Saucer" is neither gone
nor forgotten so far as the U. S. Air Force's Air Materiel Command at
Wright Field, Dayton, Ohio, is concerned.

This image is from a report in 1949 on the preliminary studies made by the Air Materiel
Command on "Flying Saucers." This is from a series of documents recently unclassified
and shows that, after years of research, the US government was unable to disprove many
of these claims.

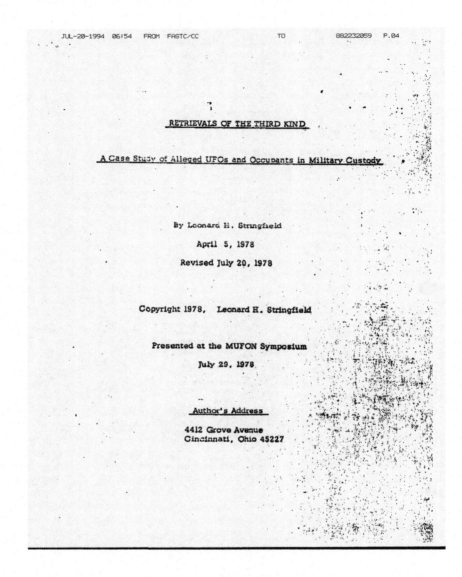

RETRIEVALS OF THE THIRD KIND

A Case Study of Alleged UFOs and Occupants in Military Custody

By Leonard H. Stringfield

April 5, 1978

Revised July 20, 1978

Copyright 1978,   Leonard H. Stringfield

Presented at the MUFON Symposium

July 29, 1978

Author's Address

4412 Grove Avenue
Cincinnati, Ohio 45227

This document shows the active participation of the US military in investigating what was called "Retrievals of the Third Kind: A Case Study of Alleged UFOs and Occupants in Military Custody." This, of course, deals with the possible contact and housing of the pilots and occupants of UFOS.

Credit: National Archives and Records Administration

In the nation's capital, radar recorded objects flying at unfathomable speeds zipping across the skies of Washington, D.C. in 1952. The nation's leaders waited with bated breath as jets were scrambled. Was this an invasion from another country? Or perhaps something completely different?

Dr. J. Allen Hynek, a scientific consultant for the project, remained a voice of reason and skepticism throughout, disputing assumptions and demanding evidence. "The UFO phenomenon, as studied by my colleagues and myself, bespeaks the action of some form of intelligence...but whence this intelligence springs...is much the question," he cautioned.[23]

But as the project progressed, the solutions seemed to get further away. Some incidents were explained as misinterpretations of natural events, while others were explained as covert military experiments. However, there remained a core of unexplained sightings, a collection of incidents that defied explanation and tested comprehension.

The detectives were balancing on a tightrope stretched across the gap of human comprehension. They were forerunners and explorers in a wilderness that refused to reveal its secrets easily.

Critics began to emerge, accusing the initiative of covering up its findings and demanding transparency. The waters became muddy, and the line between reality and fiction, truth and deception became increasingly hazy. Project Blue Book was unraveling a tapestry with no end in sight, a complicated web of sightings, events, and phenomena that presented a picture that was both fascinating and frustrating.

As time passed, the project encountered its own challenges, including questions about its methods, results, and very purpose. Would the answers ever be discovered? Or was this an enigma that would never be solved, a cosmic puzzle with no solution?

A CHRISTIAN PERSPECTIVE

As the Project Blue Book investigation delved into the physical, it also inadvertently examined the spiritual. A mysterious and enigmatic inquiry arose that transcended the earthly world: what did these unexplained happenings mean in the grand symphony of God's creation?

The scientists who led the investigation were unprepared to deal with theological consequences. These are the questions many Americans struggled with then, and many more will battle soon.

The Lubbock Lights, as well as the Washington, D.C. sightings and a slew of other inexplicable occurrences, presented a problem. Were these divine signs? Or were they a type of spiritual illusion, a charade conjured up by evil forces beyond our senses? Pastors and theologians would investigate the phenomenon and attempt to comprehend it in light of Scripture. Some interpreted these incidents as a sign of the end times.

As the argument raged on, Project Blue Book resumed its inquiry, a scientific pursuit that appeared to be becoming increasingly entwined with the paranormal.

PROJECT BLUE BOOK'S END AND UNANSWERED QUESTIONS

As the years passed, Project Blue Book—once a beacon of research and knowledge—became embroiled in controversy and uncertainty. The public's curiosity in the unknown was only matched by growing mistrust about how the government handled the problem.

Not only were questions raised about the sightings, but they were also raised about the investigation's credibility. Critics accused the project of being a smokescreen, a meticulously crafted façade designed to conceal the truth. In a complicated world, both can be true at the same time.

Dr. J. Allen Hynek, who had previously been a cautious voice inside the research, began to express his dissatisfaction. I often feel the same way because this very subject seems to draw unto itself a host of opportunists, self-seekers, crackpots, and others who muddy the waters.

The decision was reached amid rising pressure and a shifting political scene: Project Blue Book was to be terminated. The announcement was made in 1969, capping off a journey that had caught the imagination of a nation and the world. The official line was unequivocal: there was no evidence of extraterrestrial life or any threat to national security.

However, the conclusion did not put an end to the questions. It did not quench the thirst for knowledge or soothe the newly awakened feeling of cosmic curiosity. Theologians and intellectuals continued to mull over the ramifications, attempting to reconcile these UFOs or UAPs with biblical teachings.

Project Blue Book's legacy is a complicated mosaic fashioned from strands of science, theology, politics, and human curiosity. But the legacy of Project Blue Book is not confined to official archives or dusty shelves of lost history. It represents a lingering question in the hearts of millions around the world. Will the Church give them an answer, or will we allow the enemy to fill the vacuum and control the narrative?

The evolution of Dr. J. Allen Hynek from skeptical scientist to open-minded inquirer captures the spirit of this journey.

The questions it aroused have yet to be answered, the riddles go undiscovered, and the curiosity is still unsatisfied. As we ponder the legacy of Project Blue Book, we are reminded of the words of the apostle Paul in 1 Corinthians 13:12 (NIV):

> *For now we see only a reflection as in a mirror; then we shall see face to face. Now I know in part; then I shall know fully, even as I am fully known.*

CHAPTER EIGHT

THE SKINWALKER RANCH

UFO sightings and thoughtful investigations into the truth did not end with Project Blue Book. Certain places around the world have emerged as hotspots for paranormal activity and some are committed to uncovering their mysteries.

On Skinwalker Ranch—a large property in Utah's Uinta Basin, notorious for strange occurrences and disquieting events—a particular night was unusually tranquil. The ranch was dotted with scientists from the National Institute for Discovery Science (NIDS), which was funded by Robert Bigelow, a Las Vegas industrialist. Their state-of-the-art equipment was aimed at the sky and surrounding area.

Dr. Jim, the chief scientist, received a radio call at 12:03 a.m. that caused his heart to race, telling him that he needed to get to the northeast field, right away!

Ellen, his field assistant, sounded flustered over the phone. Dr. Jim rushed to his ATV and raced across the ranch's rugged landscape. As he approached the northeast field, he observed a phenomenon that was difficult to explain. Three blue spheres, approximately the size of basketballs, floated a few feet above the ground. They appeared to be moving and emitting a faint hum.

The scientists set up their equipment as fast as they could to collect as much data as possible. Suddenly, one of the spheres flew toward the group and halted just a few feet away. It lingered there for a minute, illuminating the field with an eerie blue light.

Dr. Jim claimed that in that moment fear gripped him. This is important because this sense of paralyzing fear is common among those who claim to have encountered a UFO or UAP (unidentified anomalous phenomena). Before he could move, the ball let out a high-pitched shriek and took off straight up into the air. Everyone was in shock![24]

These experiences have only increased over the years. Skinwalker Ranch has now gained international popularity and has perplexed, horrified, and fascinated observers around the world.

Our aim here isn't just to tell scary stories or common legends about Skinwalker Ranch. The Church should always investigate what the world is talking about and attempt to provide a biblical answer that stirs up hope and truth instead of fear and inuendo.

Since this is a subject that could easily lead to sensationalism and unsubstantiated rumors, it is crucial that we approach it with caution. We should always lean toward trustworthy sources, confirmed evidence, and, most importantly, a biblical lens to make sense of odd occurrences like this. We should first seek natural explanations, but also be willing to consider the inconceivable, such as the possibility that what's happening at Skinwalker Ranch is an omen of a coming spiritual war in the last days. Could the suggested narrative that circulates from places like this play into the antichrist's end-time deception?

THE SKINNY ON THE RANCH

In addition to being remote from prying eyes, Skinwalker Ranch boasts around 500 acres, and it has a lengthy history with the Utes and Navajos. These indigenous groups have revered and respected the area for centuries. According to local legend and tribal accounts, the ranch is cursed—a notion that has only grown stronger in light of the unusual events that have transpired there throughout time. The term "Skinwalker" originates from Navajo tales about evil entities who roam the land and can alter their appearance. These entities were often reported to take the shape of a human-animal hybrid and are ubiquitous in every culture throughout history. Are they just stories, or thinking back to our discussion of the Nephilim of Genesis 6, could they be a modern-day equivalent?

Long before scholars and the media became interested in the land, Native Americans and early settlers claimed the ranch was a location where bizarre incidents occurred. For years, local legends have been filled with tales of strange flying objects that resemble glowing orbs, enigmatic cattle deaths, and sightings of large, mysterious animals. Peculiar structures, such as crop circles and electrical hotspots, have also been spotted, prompting many to ponder what forces are at work on this abnormal tract of land.

The property has changed hands numerous times, with each new proprietor seemingly eager to solve its mysteries. Robert Bigelow, a Nevadan industrialist who was very interested in investigating the unexplained, is one of the most well-known. During Bigelow's oversight, there was considerable scrutiny and investigation. He recruited the NIDS, a think tank that employs scientific methods to investigate occurrences that defy natural explanation. Teams of physicists, biologists, and other scientists examined ranch life for years as part of NIDS, with frequently ambiguous or puzzling results.

As you can see, there is a complex blend of folklore, eyewitness accounts, and scientific research surrounding this area. The ranch is a mysterious location where the known and the unknown, the material and the spiritual, dance together in a manner that is difficult to completely understand.

THE SECRET OF SKINWALKER RANCH

In an era when television and the internet frequently make it difficult to determine what is real and what is not, the History Channel's series *The Secret of Skinwalker Ranch* has accomplished something remarkable: it has brought to the attention of the public a location that was previously shrouded in mystery and urban legend. Since its first episode, the program has brought a global audience to the ranch. It went from being a fringe area of study to a major pop culture phenomenon. Due to the inclusion of interviews with eyewitnesses, exhaustive research, and on-site scientific experiments, the series has developed an enthusiastic following. It has also provided the ranch's current proprietor, Brandon Fugal, with an opportunity to express his evolving views on the strange occurrences there.

The responses to the Skinwalker Ranch television program have been as diverse as they are impassioned. Fans anxiously anticipate each new episode hoping to finally have the answers. In contrast, the scientific community has been typically more skeptical. Even though it is agreed that there are unexplained phenomena at the ranch that should be investigated, critics assert that the program frequently leans toward sensationalism and undermines the credibility of actual scientific research. This skepticism is not unwarranted, given the ranch's flamboyant history and the difficulty of obtaining reliable information from such tales. I'll leave it up to you to determine how the show handles all of this, but it sure is entertaining to watch. It appears that the team they have assembled has done an amazing job of investigating the mysteries surrounding the ranch.

This tension between belief and skepticism, between the popular and the scientific, is what keeps the Skinwalker Ranch mystery alive and intriguing. In any case, this location has made its way into the mainstream, and the Church should be ready to provide well-informed and thought-out answers to the inevitable questions believers are going to ask. But what does the current owner say about his curious acquisition?

THE CURRENT OWNER

When affluent businessman and real estate mogul Brandon Fugal purchased Skinwalker Ranch in 2016, it marked a significant turning point in the ranch's history. Fugal wasn't simply another affluent land buyer; he added a new dimension to the ranch's complicated story. He purchased the ranch because he was skilled in business and intrigued by the unknown. This resulted in a renewed endeavor to investigate the strange occurrences at the ranch using both scientific methods and an openness to spiritual explanations. Fugal has since invested a great deal of money and time investigating the ranch's mysteries. He has purchased high-tech equipment and hired specialists in numerous disciplines.

During his tenure as proprietor of Skinwalker Ranch, Brandon Fugal's perspective on the strange occurrences has evolved gradually. Initially, it appears that he was simply interested in scientific research, but his observations and experiences have led him to believe that the ranch may be a place where something more than UFOs are operating. While maintaining his interest in science, he has stated in various interviews that the things he has witnessed—which range from difficult to explain to genuinely terrifying—could be interpreted as spiritual warfare. I'm paraphrasing, but this is essentially what he has said, and I believe he is correct.

Brandon Fugal has consequently introduced into the discussion of Skinwalker Ranch topics that are typically taboo or forbidden in secular study. He urges both believers and skeptics to look past what they already know and adopt a multidimensional approach that considers both scientific facts and spiritual understanding.

In a recent interview, ex-pentagon official and UAP taskforce member Luis Elizondo came out and said that a senior Department of Defense (DOD) official told him that UFOs were not extraterrestrial but demonic.[25] He even told him that if you read the Bible, you'll know what we're dealing with. This is a huge story that no one is covering!

EXTRATERRESTRIAL OR INTERDIMENSIONAL?

There are numerous accounts in the Bible that resemble what has occurred at Skinwalker Ranch and other places around the world. In the Old and New Testaments, both divine and demonic forces manifest in peculiar ways. The prophet Ezekiel's encounter with a celestial chariot, Daniel's battle with territorial spirits, and Jesus' many exorcisms all demonstrate that the universe is full of spiritual beings that interact with the physical world.

Consider the "Legion" incident from Mark 5:5-13 (KJV), in which Jesus encounters a man possessed by many demons:

> *And always, night and day, he was in the mountains, and in the tombs, crying, and cutting himself with*

stones. But when he saw Jesus afar off, he ran and worshipped him, and cried with a loud voice, and said, What have I to do with thee, Jesus, thou Son of the most high God? I adjure thee by God, that thou torment me not. For he said unto him, Come out of the man, thou unclean spirit.

And he asked him, What is thy name? And he answered, saying, My name is Legion: for we are many. And he besought him much that he would not send them away out of the country. Now there was there nigh unto the mountains a great herd of swine feeding. And all the devils besought him, saying, Send us into the swine, that we may enter into them. And forthwith Jesus gave them leave. And the unclean spirits went out, and entered into the swine: and the herd ran violently down a steep place into the sea, (they were about two thousand;) and were choked in the sea.

This narrative describes not only a form of possession, but also the ability of these creatures to influence the physical environment, even drowning a herd of swine. If you believe the Bible to be true, it's not unreasonable to believe that certain events at Skinwalker Ranch could be the work of malevolent forces. Fallen angels, Nephilim, and malevolent technology are all covered in the Bible.

Could the increase in odd occurrences today be a sign of an increase in spiritual activity as the "last days" approach? Has spiritual activity increased because the enemy knows his time is short?

Therefore rejoice, ye heavens, and ye that dwell in them. Woe to the inhabiters of the earth and of the sea! for the devil is come down unto you, having great wrath, because he knoweth that he hath but a short time (Revelation 12:12 KJV).

Balance is essential. However, it does not seem prudent to completely rule out demonic activity. What many suppose to be extraterrestrial may just be interdimensional entities. Both angels and demons fit into this category.

WHY YOU MUST EXERCISE CAUTION

Skinwalker Ranch is a labyrinth of mysteries, and any topic that opens the door to preternatural or paranormal occurrences must be approached with caution.

> *Test the spirits to see whether they are from God* (1 John 4:1 NIV).

Our journey into the unknown should not be a leap into the darkness, but rather a cautious step into the illumination of God's Word. If you stray too far from God's Word, you could unwittingly invite demonic activity into your own life. Stick close to Jesus. It is essential to approach this topic with an open mind, but an open mind should never become an empty mind. To be able to discern what corresponds with God's truth and what does not, we must fill our minds with biblical truth, theological insights, and divine counsel.

> *And no marvel; for Satan himself is transformed into an angel of light* (2 Corinthians 11:14 KJV).

Remember, even satan presents himself as an angel of light, and his demons are very skilled at manipulating the masses. Without prudence, we may be exposed to spiritual and doctrinal issues that are as hazardous as they are alluring. We must not only teach what the Bible says about these entities, but also how you can exercise authority over them in the name of Jesus.

HOW THE CHURCH OPERATES

As the "pillar and foundation of truth" (see 1 Timothy 3:15), the Church plays a crucial role in these discussions. When the Church is reticent or uninterested in such significant issues, it can leave a void that is quickly filled with rumors, superstitions, and non-biblical views. Any involvement without a solid grasp of theology can lead to sensationalism and a diversion from the central message of the Gospel.

The Church must act responsibly, providing a biblically based perspective that does not disregard or exaggerate strange occurrences like those at Skinwalker Ranch. By doing so, the Church can present a balanced perspective consistent with biblical truth, while also acknowledging that God's world is enigmatic and complex. In a culture obsessed with the mystical and unexplainable, the Church has the unique responsibility of continually directing people back to Christ, the Alpha and Omega:

> *In whom are hidden all the treasures of wisdom and knowledge* (Colossians 2:3 NIV).

We may not understand strange phenomena that occur, but there is One who does. Any attempt to explain the unusual occurrences in our world should bring us closer to Christ, who alone can explain both the ordinary and the extraordinary. Jesus and the Holy Spirit are our only reliable sources for direction.

The Church can be a beacon in a world captivated with mysteries by approaching these occurrences with scholarly rigor and spiritual discernment, always pointing the way back to Christ, our secure foundation and ultimate authority in all things visible and invisible. Our journey through the odd occurrences at Skinwalker Ranch teaches that we must remain vigilant when attempting to comprehend the world around us. As the guardian of truth, the Church plays a crucial role in these debates, directing both believers and skeptics back to enduring Gospel truths.

ALIEN INTERROGATION?

I recently did an interview with an investigator who claims to have video footage of an actual alien interrogation. We showed the video on our Encounter Today program and discussed the possibilities. It's fascinating! Why would I allow such a strange conversation on my Christian program? It's not because I'm convinced the video is real. I'll let you be the judge of that. It's because these are the questions the world is asking, and I want them to find answers in the house of God.

QUESTIONS YOU MUST CONSIDER

Consider how what we've discussed in this chapter may alter or expand your understanding of spiritual warfare, demons, and the essence of evil in our world. How does it align with or differ from the Bible's teachings on malevolent forces? How should Christians interact with media outlets that explore the supernatural?

As Christians living in a world that is increasingly fascinated by the bizarre and supernatural, what guidelines should we follow when viewing or reading about these topics? How can we and those around us prepare to approach these topics with an open mind and a watchful heart? May this investigation not only serve as an intellectual exercise, but also as a spiritual journey that brings us closer to the heart of God and His plan for our victory in Jesus Christ in these last days.

CHAPTER NINE

CLOSE ENCOUNTERS OR DEMON POSSESSION?

Close encounters with alien entities have been a subject that has consistently captivated the public's attention. Reports of encounters with extraterrestrial creatures have become a cultural obsession, from eerie kidnappings to odd nighttime sightings. Shows like *Fire in the Sky*, *The Fourth Kind*, and *The X-Files* depict terrifying reenactments of alleged incidents, imprinting them on our collective psyche. But what if there's more to these encounters than just extraterrestrial curiosity? What if these contacts are not the result of distant aliens, but of a more sinister and spiritual reality?

The theory that extraterrestrial encounters may be integrally related to demonic possession is not new, but it is frequently marginalized. It's either too spiritual or not complicated enough to interest those who are always looking for a "new thing." However, a remarkable pattern that cannot be ignored is shown when the data, testimonials, and commonalities between these incidents are examined. In their 1992 book *The Facts on UFOs and Other Supernatural Phenomena*, Drs. John Ankerberg and John Weldon explore the connections between UFO sightings and spiritual deception, providing a glimpse into the spiritual warfare that may lie behind these encounters.

Are these alleged experiences with extraterrestrial entities merely the product of an overactive imagination, verifiable contact with extraterrestrial life, or something else entirely? The solutions might contradict our preconceptions, make us reevaluate how we perceive the world, and strengthen our confidence in the Creator, who gives us authority over all devils:

> *Behold, I give unto you power to tread on serpents and scorpions, and over all the power of the enemy: and nothing shall by any means hurt you* (Luke 10:19 KJV).

This is a journey of discernment, a quest for truth, and an investigation of the invisible spiritual battlefield. It is a call to identify the true enemy, empower ourselves with God's Word, and maintain our composure in the face of supernatural lies.

The manifestations depicted in "close encounter" stories are remarkably similar to descriptions of demonic possession and spiritual oppression documented throughout Christian literature. The paralysis, manipulation, fear, and spiritual unrest mirror symptoms described by exorcists and spiritual warfare experts.

Respected Christian academics and theologians have investigated the relationship between extraterrestrial encounters and demonic possession. Dr. Michael Heiser explores the historical foundations of spiritual deceit in his book *Reversing Hermon: Enoch, the Watchers, and the Forgotten Mission of Jesus Christ*, published in 2017. The comparisons between the tales in Nome, Alaska, and the biblical notion of demonic creatures is astounding and too similar to be ignored.

Abduction stories serve as sobering case studies into spiritual warfare. The evidence, the testimonies, and the spiritual consequences all point to a reality that goes beyond just an interest in aliens. Could it be that the people who experienced these encounters were engaged in a spiritual conflict with demonic forces rather than being held captive by aliens?

ALIEN ABDUCTIONS AND DEMONIC OPPRESSION

There is a recurring and unsettling trend in the accounts of people being abducted by supernatural beings from their beds, cars, or peaceful forest pathways. As mentioned before, those who claim to have been abducted often exhibit symptoms that are eerily similar to those of others who have experienced demonic oppression. Paralysis, inability to cry out or move, and an overpowering sensation of dread and panic are all experienced by victims of demonic attack and alien abduction alike. They talk about lost time, experiences that seem both real and dreamlike, and a sense of being mistreated by forces they can neither comprehend nor fight. People who have experienced such spiritual assaults describe being unable to move or talk, as well as intense fear that goes beyond normal apprehension or trepidation. The similarities are too obvious to ignore.

Another aspect that connects these two occurrences is that of manipulation and deception. Many abductees report feeling duped or manipulated by the aliens they interact with. In John 8:43-45 (KJV), satan is called the father of lies:

> Why do ye not understand my speech? even because ye cannot hear my word. Ye are of your father the devil, and the lusts of your father ye will do. He was a murderer from the beginning, and abode not in the truth,

because there is no truth in him. When he speaketh a lie, he speaketh of his own: for he is a liar, and the father of it. And because I tell you the truth, ye believe me not.

Another place where the distinction between the extraterrestrial and demonic dissolves is in the physical and spiritual anguish that accompanies these abductions. Physical aches, nightmares, and a persistent feeling of spiritual disturbance that follows them long after contact are all described by abductees. Demonic oppression victims frequently speak of long-lasting bodily and spiritual ramifications, which is evidence of the significant influence these experiences can have.

The well-known UFO researcher Dr. Jacques Vallée offers a fascinating viewpoint on these linkages. In his book, *Passport to Magonia: From Folklore to Flying Saucers* from 1969, Vallée examines the connections between contemporary UFO sightings and past claims of encounters with extraterrestrial life. His comparisons bring out the spiritual aspects of the situation even more, connecting the modern and the mystical. Both alien abductions and demonic oppression involve deception, manipulation, and fear. This points to a fight that goes beyond the physical world.

The overlapping of these two events calls into question the conventional view of alien encounters. It encourages us to view these encounters as representations of an invisible, spiritual conflict rather than merely a physical contact with extraterrestrial beings. In fact, we might be more accurate by calling them interdimensional instead of extraterrestrial. This is perfectly in line with what the Bible teaches about these fallen entities.

SPIRITUAL FORCES OF EVIL?

Furthermore, several victims of abduction claim that calling on the name of Jesus Christ ended their traumatic encounter. This powerful spiritual link is highlighted by renowned UFO researcher Joe Jordan, who collated more than 400 similar incidents. His research, which is detailed in *Unholy Communion: The Alien Abduction Phenomenon, Where It Originates and How It Stops*, provides strong proof that these experiences are not only chance encounters but are instead deliberate spiritual assaults.[26] These stories are not singular outliers. The phenomenon of alien encounters and the ominous world of demonic activities are connected by a pattern they produce, a recurrent thread. All the signs, signals, and tactics lead to an interdimensional conflict and have a spiritual resonance with age-old spiritual truths.

Though the deceiver's strategies may have changed over time, his objectives have not: to mislead, to instill fear, and to sever people from their faith in God. Paul the apostle said:

> For our struggle is not against flesh and blood, but against the rulers, against the authorities, against the powers of this dark world and against the **spiritual forces of evil** in the heavenly realms (Ephesians 6:12 NIV).

This is just as true today as it ever was. The nature of these interactions urges us to delve below the surface, past the sensationalism, and into the spiritual reality that underlies our existence in a world obsessed with the mysterious.

BEYOND THE SURFACE:
EXAMPLES OF ALIEN ENCOUNTERS
AS DEMONIC MANIFESTATIONS

The search for a link between alien encounters and demonic forces extends beyond the frigid Alaskan tundra of Nome or the eerie deserts of Roswell. Similar tales have spread across continents and civilizations, creating a tangled web of deception.

1. The Hill Abduction: 1961

In the middle of the 20th century, the story of Betty and Barney Hill[27] was the talk of the world. The pair described a terrifying experience in which they were carried aboard a UFO, put through medical tests, and had contact with extraterrestrial beings. The characteristics of these aliens, their purposes, and the lingering repercussions on the Hills, however, bear a frightening resemblance to experiences with demons. The bizarre symbols, the immobility they felt that fateful night, and Betty's violent dreams all fit the description—provided by trained exorcists—of spiritual oppression.

It was a dark and stormy night in September of 1961. After visiting Montreal, Canada, Betty and Barney Hill were making their way back to Portsmouth, New Hampshire. They simply wanted to return home since they were worn out and exhausted from their trip.

They noticed a dazzling light in the sky as they traveled through the rural countryside. The light seemed to be following them and was moving erratically. Betty and Barney were becoming increasingly concerned. To observe the light, they stopped their vehicle on the side of the road. The Hills got out of their car to investigate when the light ultimately landed in a clearing.

When they got closer to it, they noticed that the light was coming from a sizable oval-shaped ship. They had never seen anything like the craft before. They said that it had a row of windows and was sleek and silver. The Hills were too scared to move. They were unsure about what to do. The ship's entrance suddenly opened, and a ramp lowered to the ground.

They testified that small, human-like beings started to emerge from the craft. The creatures had enormous heads, almond-shaped eyes, and were around four feet tall. They had odd objects in their hands and wore silver outfits.

The aliens motioned for them to follow them as they approached the Hills. Although the Hills were afraid, they felt that they had no other options. Into the spaceship they went, along with the beings. The ship launched itself into the night sky. Strange things happened to the Hills on their trip. They were given a star chart to look over and had a physical examination. The biology of the Hills seemed to be of interest to the aliens. They collected samples of their blood and hair, and they used odd machines to scan their bodies.

The craft eventually touched down back in the clearing. The Hills were freed and instructed to keep their experiences private. They didn't discuss what had transpired for a long time as they made their way home in quiet. But the incident had permanently altered them. Both experienced dreams and visions of the aliens. Additionally, they started to have bodily issues including headaches and exhaustion.

The Hills tried hypnosis a year after the kidnapping in an effort to regain their memory of what happened (not a good solution). When she was hypnotized, Betty was able to give a thorough explanation of what had occurred. Her story matched Barney's memories, which he had independently rediscovered.

The Hill abduction is one of the most well-known and well-documented alien abduction cases. Numerous books, articles, and television documentaries have touched on it. Some people think the Hills' narrative is real; others think it's a fabrication.

2. Operation Saucer: 1977

It was 1977, and something strange was brewing in the little, isolated village of Colares, Brazil. There were rumors among the locals of spectral lights dancing over the Amazon River, haunting apparitions in the night sky, and rays that could pierce human flesh. These were not just scary stories for kids; these were tales from farmers, fishermen, and even doctors. As the sightings grew, a chill of dread descended upon the neighborhood.

A file labeled "Operation Saucer" was opened in the heart of the Brazilian Air Force's headquarters. The formal inquiry by the Brazilian Air Force was prompted by a peculiar series of events. Residents claimed physical injuries, attacks by glowing objects, and a palpable panic that engulfed entire towns. This phenomenon shared similarities with demonic manifestations, including manipulation, physical harm, and the induction of fear and chaos.

The man recognized for his analytical mind and calm demeanor, Captain Uyrangê Hollanda, was called to investigate the Colares phenomenon, uncover the facts, and put an end to the mounting dread.

With a crew of skilled investigators and a vehicle loaded with cameras, radars, and scientific equipment, Captain Hollanda and his crew landed in Colares. They were hailed by the townspeople, who had mixed emotions of hope and horror in their eyes. They talked about the "Chupa-Chupa," the strange lights that tormented their nights and left some of their neighbors traumatized.

The crew patrolled every night with cameras primed, senses at the ready. They spoke with eyewitnesses whose hands shook as they described what they had seen. They looked at the wounds, which were very precise and severe.

Then it happened. A light appeared in the black night sky. It pulsed and moved in unnatural patterns over the river. As he gave his crew the go-ahead, Captain Hollanda could feel his heart pounding in his chest. Radars beeped, cameras clicked, and notebooks were crammed with frenzied notes. After a tense standoff, the light finally disappeared into the night after appearing to be aware that it was being observed.

Days became weeks, and then weeks became months. More sightings came but no conclusive solutions. Not only were the mysterious lights watching the squad, but so were their supervisors, who demanded results. In the end, the official study didn't come to a final conclusion. It had a lot of information but no answers. The file was closed; the team was disbanded. However, Captain Hollanda was aware that they had encountered something incomprehensible, something that hinted at a reality that was both bigger and more mysterious than anyone dared to acknowledge.

Operation Saucer's once-secret files were made public years later, but the truth was still hard to find, hidden under layers of secrecy and ambiguity. What did Colares' lights represent? Who or what intelligence guided them? Operation Saucer's unanswered questions remain a perplexing puzzle that begs to be solved yet has resisted all attempts so far.

SPIRITUAL WARFARE IN MODERN TIMES

As it becomes more and more evident that alien encounters could actually be caused by demonic behavior, we must think about how

Christians should react. We must be able to participate in this spiritual conflict; simply acknowledging its existence is not enough. We must take authority over it in Jesus' Name. The apostle Peter admonishes us:

> *Be sober, be watchful: your adversary the devil, as a roaring lion, walketh about, seeking whom he may devour* (1 Peter 5:8 ASV).

This is just as relevant today as it ever was. But how do we arm ourselves—and others around us—for such a conflict? The wisdom of Ephesians and James has the solution. In Ephesians 6:11 (NIV), believers are urged to put on all of God's armor to resist the devil's plans:

> *Put on the full armor of God, so that you can take your stand against the devil's schemes.*
>
> *Submit yourselves therefore to God. Resist the devil, and he will flee from you* (James 4:7 KJV).

To combat these supernatural deceptions, the Church must act as a bulwark of spiritual power and a haven where Christians can find instruction, direction, and discipleship. The question might be asked, how do we resist the devil? We must return to the Word of God and learn to resist the devil in the same way Jesus did. Do you remember when Jesus had a close encounter with an alien entity who temped him in the wilderness? After satan had presented his temptations to Jesus, the Messiah responded by quoting the Word of God to him:

> *Then saith Jesus unto him, Get thee hence, Satan: for it is written, Thou shalt worship the Lord thy God, and*

*him only shalt thou serve. Then the devil leaveth him,
and, behold, angels came and ministered unto him*
(Matthew 4:10-11 KJV).

With this understanding of these "close encounters" another question arises: how do we minister to those who are tormented by these deceptions? To interact with persons who have gone through these situations, one must have both a compassionate heart, a firm belief in the Gospel's message of truth, as well as an understanding of their authority in Christ. As UFO religions and alien encounters increase in the last days, should we consider holding deliverance and healing services just for those who have been oppressed or harmed by these demonic entities?

On thing is certain and that is that we need to be a voice of hope, announcing Christ's victory amid these unusual and frightening circumstances. The fight has already been won. According to 1 John 3:8 (NLV):

The Son of God came to destroy the works of the devil.

We find our victory and our hope in Jesus. The strange, the unfathomable, and the otherworldly may draw a lot of attention, but our reaction must be based on the Bible, characterized by discernment, and guided by the Holy Spirit:

*For God hath not given us the spirit of fear; but of power,
and of love, and of a sound mind* (2 Timothy 1:7 KJV).

In our contemporary age, because people's desire for the "new" and uncharted frequently leads them to the wrong things, we must be the voice of Truth. They need to know that the Lord is our sanctuary,

His Word is our source of knowledge, and His eternal promises are our basis of victory. The war has already been won!

NAVIGATING THE UNKNOWN

The accounts and supporting documentation provided here are not merely tales of the unknown, but rather moving reminders of an ongoing spiritual conflict that is both visible and invisible. These tales, though extraordinary, reflect a universal conflict that cuts across all boundaries of time, space, and culture. They serve as a reminder that the spiritual realm is not limited to ancient literature but is a living reality in our current society. It is a reality that calls for our focus, discernment, and unflinching adherence to the truths we cherish.

We are not allowed to roam aimlessly in the shadows of uncertainty as Christ's followers. We must react to these troubling encounters with faith rather than fear, wisdom rather than awe, and compassion rather than curiosity. In a world full of dark corners and delusions, we must be the salt and light. In a day when the truth is frequently distorted and obscured, we must be its bearers.

Make this investigation a beginning rather than a conclusion, a start to a more thorough comprehension, a more profound faith, and a renewed dedication to the mission given to us. It should serve as a motivator for prayer, study, outreach, and a life of humble obedience to the One who is in control of all.

TRUTH IN THE DARK

We have traveled together into the center of a mystery that tests not only our comprehension of the world, but also our own souls in the swirl of doubt and deception around the phenomenon of alien contacts and its relationship to demonic manifestations.

Let's resolve not to be swayed by sensationalism or fear but rather to proceed in confidence, equipped with the Word of God, led by the Spirit, and rooted in the love of Christ.

CHAPTER TEN

PROJECT BLUE BEAM:
The Genesis
of a Conspiracy Theory

A tale that is as contentious as it is intriguing emerges from the shadowy recesses of contemporary legend, where fact and fiction converge. A tale that suggests a large-scale fraud, a world conspiracy, and a technological marvel intended to usher in a new era—or perhaps signal the end of the world. This is the story of Project Blue Beam.

In 1994, the globe was on the cusp of a new millennium and was filled with both excitement and trepidation. During this combustible period, a Canadian journalist, Serge Monast, disclosed to the globe an audacious, intricately devised plot that would send shockwaves through the decades. Though we do not follow after conspiracy theories, it has resurfaced recently. It seems to continue to gain momentum, which is why it's important for you to know the truth behind it.

In his works, Monast described a plot by a covert international organization to bring about a new world order by simulating the Second Coming of Christ or an alien invasion—a scheme that, if carried out, would upend all reason and belief in our modern world.[28]

The assertion was strong, but the proof was scant. It was quickly dismissed by critics as fiction and the babbling of a mind gripped by anxiety and fear. Political science professors like Dr. Michael Barkun who authored *A Culture of Conspiracy* may say that Project Blue Beam lacks evidence and builds on unfounded fears.[29] However, the idea has lingered and served as a warning, a prophecy, and a call to vigilance for those who believed in it, especially in a society where the distinction between truth and falsehood was becoming increasingly hazy.

So, what was Project Blue Beam? Was it merely a story fashioned from strands of fear and imagination? Or was it a revelation, a window into the covert workings of power and influence? We must exercise caution as we explore the shadows because, for whatever reason, conspiracy theories like these appear to be addictive. Have you noticed how people can go down these rabbit holes, and it can feed an unhealthy mindset? It feeds distrust, and the enemy has a field day in the minds of those who are not disciplined enough to stay grounded in the Word.

Are we capable of looking beyond the seen with boldness and courage knowing that:

> *Greater is he that is in you, than he that is in the world*
> (1 John 4:4 KJV).

The meticulous architecture of Project Blue Beam, which unfolds in four unique stages, is what makes it distinctive. Each stage serves as a stepping-stone toward a global transformation and is part of a puzzle that, when put together, creates a picture of deception and control, faith and delusion.

STAGE ONE:
ARTIFICIAL ARCHAEOLOGICAL FINDS

This first stage of Blue Beam asserts that global elites will create massive earthquakes or natural disasters that will unearth *new* archeological treasures. These new finds will conveniently disprove modern religious beliefs and shake the foundations of major world religions. These discoveries will speak of the need of one-world religion. The age-old argument between faith and archaeology is manipulated, challenging the deeply held beliefs of millions.

An eminent archaeologist, Dr. William Dever, stated, "Archaeological data can illuminate the historical context of the biblical narratives; to think it can (or should) prove or disprove miracles is, again, to miss the point."[30] Though I believe that archaeology absolutely proves the accuracy of the Word of God, this is an interesting point, especially when faced with the possibility of false archeological finds.

STAGE TWO:
THE GREAT SPACE SHOW

It's suggested here that holograms of religious figures or apocalyptic events will be projected onto the sky to create a spectacular spectacle, a celestial theater, and an all-encompassing religious experience. In this stage the world will be convinced that this is the end and that the true messiah has come. There are those who have argued that the requisite technology to make this happen, including 3D optical holograms and sound, goes beyond what is currently possible. However, as we have learned, with AI this could change very quickly.

The Orson Welles Radio Transmission

Could this kind of deception actually work? Hold that thought as we step back into history for a moment and consider the effect that a single radio broadcast had on society in the late 1930s. Broadcast television was still in its infancy; most people still relied on radio for news and entertainment. On the evening of October 30, 1938, millions of Americans turned on their radios in search of an entertaining distraction, only to get caught up in a web of panic and uncertainty instead. Even without visuals, the widespread effect of this transmission was astonishing.

Orson Welles, the mastermind behind the broadcast, unleashed an extraterrestrial invasion story that would become one of the most discussed media events in history. The execution and the aftermath of this phony invasion show how easily the masses can be caught up in outrageous and unbelievable narratives.

The Transmission:

Orson Welles and his Mercury Theatre on the Air dramatized H.G. Wells' *The War of the Worlds*. Orson structured the story as a sequence of breaking news bulletins, complete with realistic sound effects and a manufactured sense of urgency, rather than a standard dramatization. The performance began with what appeared to be a regular music show, only to be cut short by disturbing claims of extraterrestrial beings descending on Earth. The realism was remarkable, and many listeners were sucked in.

The Reaction:

- **Panic**—those who listened halfway through the broadcast and missed the disclaimer that it was fiction were caught off guard. Reports of individuals fainting, fleeing their homes, or phoning the police presented a picture of widespread panic.

- **Outrage**—when it became clear that the invasion was a hoax, many people felt betrayed and enraged. Welles was chastised by the media and public figures for his irresponsible use of the radio.

- **Fascination**—the show was highly praised for its inventiveness and the psychological insight it brought into crowd behavior. Psychologists and sociologists investigated the incident as a one-of-a-kind example of public reaction to media manipulation.

The Observation:

The impact of Orson Welles' broadcast provides significant insight on the power of media and the public's vulnerability to manipulation. It is a sobering reminder of how easily we can be deceived by fake news stories.

The War of the Worlds by H.G. Wells is both a testament to the power of storytelling and a warning about the impact of media on public consciousness. It speaks to current worries about fake news, deception, and the ability to distinguish truth in a cluttered media ecosystem. The masterfully designed and executed fake extraterrestrial invasion invites us to consider our own responsibilities to engage media with wisdom and judgment.

It's a story that inspires us to question everything. Perhaps, this distrust and cynicism has been the enemy's goal all along. There's no doubt it's working. If something as simple as a low-tech radio broadcast could deceive masses of people in the 1930s, how much easier would it be for rogue powers to use AI to recreate this kind of hysteria in the near future?

STAGE THREE: TELEPATHIC COMMUNICATION

Back to our look into Project Blue Beam. Both the manipulation of information surrounding archeological finds and the potential to create hysteria through mass communication have been considered as potential avenues to control the public at large. At this stage now, it's asserted that telepathic technological two-way communication will be deployed to cause delusions and influence thoughts. This is a form of manipulative mind control. Psychological warfare is expertly employed, delving into our deepest fears and desires.

Some psychologists at the time suggested that the concept of mass telepathic manipulation was far-fetched and lacked empirical support. But this was long before the military developed the "Voice of God" technology. I think now they might change their tune.

In an age in which technical developments are accelerating at an unprecedented rate, one innovation stands out for its uncanny resemblance to Project Blue Beam's prophetic warnings: "the Voice of God" technology. The device known as "the Voice of God" is a type of Long-Range Acoustic Device (LRAD) or directed acoustic weapon that can broadcast noises and voices to particular targets. It allows operators to convey messages, directives, or other auditory signals to a specific place without anybody else hearing them by focusing sound waves in a highly directed manner. Various military and law enforcement agencies have used the technology for crowd control, non-lethal deterrent, and psychological operations.

In this third stage, Serge Monast's Project Blue Beam proposes a series of manufactured events aimed at establishing a New World Order, brought about by a fabricated spiritual event or a fraudulent second coming of Christ. The project's third stage focuses on the use of telecommunication technologies to produce audio and visual illusions of divine communication.

"The Voice of God" aimed to create realistic, tailored audio illusions or simulated voices. It might possibly be used to fool people or organizations into believing they are getting direct communication from a higher power by projecting voices that claim heavenly origin.

In stage three, visuals would be employed to create a cohesive sensory illusion. When paired with "the Voice of God," the technology becomes a potent instrument for recreating spiritual experiences. This technology's precision and realism can have tremendous psychological consequences, altering ideas, behaviors, and emotions.

Well-respected ministers like David Jeremiah have been warning us of these antichrist technologies for some time. The technological ability to mimic the voice of God is a chilling reminder of the deceptions that lie ahead.

With its exact sound projection capabilities, "the Voice of God" technology is more than just a military breakthrough; it is a symbol of the complicated interplay between technology and population manipulation. Its link to Project Blue Beam's stage three demonstrates the very real ability to deceive on an unthinkable scale.

STAGE FOUR: UNIVERSAL SUPERNATURAL MANIFESTATIONS

The third phase devolves into the paranormal with the purported orchestration of events to convince people that an alien invasion is imminent and that there is a need for immediate world unification. The idea touches on subjects that have captivated people for ages. The truth is that our attraction to the unknown and supernatural has been a part of the human psyche since the beginning. It resonates with our deepest yearnings and our darkest fears. The global elites want to create a global threat that will encourage us to join the global solution—a one-world government.

As we examine the specifics, we are left with uncertainties. How likely are these stages to occur? Where does reality end and fantasy begin? Can technology really influence people's beliefs on such a large scale?

CHRISTIAN PERSPECTIVE AND THEOLOGICAL REFLECTIONS

Project Blue Beam is more than just a story of world conspiracy and technological wonder. Biblical warnings concerning false prophets and deception in the end times are brought to mind by the notion of this grand illusion, a spectacle designed to confuse and control. Jesus Himself issued a warning, saying:

> *For false Christs and false prophets will arise and will show great signs and wonders, so as to mislead, if possible, even the elect* (Matthew 24:24 NASB).

The underlying theme running through Project Blue Beam resonates with this Christian understanding of the end-time deception. This is why it's much easier for Christians to give conspiracy theories like this the time of day.

If Project Blue Beam begins to unfold, its conspirators will seek to directly challenge the Christian faith through fictitious archaeological discoveries. These discoveries will challenge the truthfulness and veracity of the Bible. Our faith must not be rooted in dead religion but in a personal relationship with Jesus. We cannot trust in historical relics or dogmas. If we don't discuss these things, as farfetched as they may seem, how can we expect the average Christian to be prepared? Our faith must be able to stand the trials that are coming to the earth.

Speaking of the end times, the prophet Jeremiah prophesied that the bones of the past would be unearthed and placed on display. The purpose of this display of bones was ostensibly to highlight the sins of those who did not follow God. It could easily be distorted and twisted by the enemy to fit the dialogue of the Blue Beam project. Whose bones were these, really, and where did they come from? Was this an alien encampment of old? Were these the bones of aliens who worshipped the sun, moon, and stars—indicating their extraplanetary origin?

Or would the treatment of these bones foreshadow the treatment of any who resisted a one-world order?

> At that time, saith the Lord, they shall bring out the bones of the kings of Judah, and the bones of his princes, and the bones of the priests, and the bones of the prophets, and the bones of the inhabitants of Jerusalem, out of their graves: and they shall spread them before the sun, and the moon, and all the host of

heaven, whom they have loved, and whom they have served (Jeremiah 8:1-2 KJV).

This theory's purported technological achievements highlight the ongoing conflict between science and theology. Can supernatural experiences be duplicated or controlled by human technology? What moral and spiritual ramifications result from this? Researchers like Dr. Alister McGrath, a prominent Christian scholar, highlight the potential dangers of technological advancement without moral and spiritual guidance.[31]

Global unification under a one-world government, which is Project Blue Beam's alleged ultimate goal, is reminiscent of doomsday predictions and cautionary stories all throughout the Bible about the perils of unification without divine direction. The Tower of Babel offers a case in point:

> *And the Lord said, Behold, the people is one, and they have all one language; and this they begin to do: and now nothing will be restrained from them, which they have imagined to do. Go to, let us go down, and there confound their language, that they may not understand one another's speech* (Genesis 11:6-7 KJV).

Renowned eschatologist Dr. John Walvoord compares the drive for a global unity to the Tower of Babel and says that it's a lesson in human pride. It challenges us to consider our personal convictions, our judgment, and our readiness to live in a world where deceptions can be created and the truth can be perverted.[32]

> *But sanctify the Lord God in your hearts: and be ready always to give an answer to every man that asketh you*

a reason of the hope that is in you with meekness and fear (1 Peter 3:15 KJV).

Despite being cloaked in mystery and mistrust, the mythology of Project Blue Beam serves as a parable for the times we live in. It serves as a mirror, reflecting our distrust in all the agencies that control society, and reinforces our need for a biblically based faith.

THE CRITIQUE: FACT, FICTION, OR FEAR?

The boundaries between fact and fiction are frequently hazy in the realm of conspiracy theories. The extravagant promises and complex architecture of Project Blue Beam have drawn admirers and detractors, sparking contentious discussions and probing inquiries.

Project Blue Beam's technological innovations, which range from extensive holographic projections to widespread telepathic contact, are clearly ambitious. Are they nonetheless feasible? It is both exciting and disturbing to consider how one could influence human thought on a large scale. What psychological concepts could support such an effort, and is it even possible?

Experts in human memory and cognition like Dr. Elizabeth Loftus have often shared how the idea of implanting specific thoughts or beliefs in a mass population is an overreach of our current understanding of human psychology, but recent history says otherwise. From the rise of fascism in Germany to recent global virus hysteria, we can see how populations can be easily manipulated. *Mass Formation Psychosis* is a term often applied to the idea of influencing and controlling public thought on a mass scale. Though not technically a diagnosis, it can be understood—in a political sense—to refer to the vulnerability of a group of people having their thoughts about a certain person, subject, or event manipulated to the point that they all perceive the matter in the same way, be it positively or negatively.

What does the Project Blue Beam theory indicate about the historical, cultural, and social dynamics and why did it develop at the time it occurred?

THE INFLUENCE OF SERGE MONAST

Analyzing Project Blue Beam reveals a nuanced interaction between science, psychology, history, theology, and a person's charisma. The theory's longevity could simply be a testament to its emotional resonance and capacity to capture contemporary trends as well as basic human concerns. Or it could be that we're seeing portions of it played out right before our eyes.

The questions, however, remain as we sort through the evidence. Is Project Blue Beam a real threat, a hoax, or possibly a metaphorical reflection of deeper concerns and desires? Can we dismiss it as simple fiction, or does it cause us to think more deeply about our time and our beliefs on who is running the world?

ARREST AND MYSTERIOUS DEATH: THE FINAL DAYS OF SERGE MONAST

Serge Monast's final chapter began with an occurrence as disturbing as the theories he promoted. Monast found himself in a predicament that would quickly become tragic after being arrested and having to deal with the legal system. His death, which happened right after he was arrested, has become a source of suspicion and mystery, just like the riddles he was trying to solve.

Monast was detained in 1996 for reasons that have been seriously questioned. According to some reports, the arrest was related to his research efforts and was an attempt to quell his increasingly loud revelations concerning Project Blue Beam. Others make references to the charges' more individualized and formal nature. The specifics are still unclear, clouded by uncertainty.

According to witnesses, the arrest itself was sudden and conducted with an intensity that startled them. Although Monast was detained and then freed, the encounter left him disturbed and, according to his close friends, extremely afraid for his life. Serge Monast passed away from what was formally identified as a heart attack a few days after his arrest. The timing seemed ominous and the situation perplexing. Here was a man who had been diving into the shadows, revealing what he believed to be world-changing conspiracies, and now he was gone.

Some reports claim that Monast's relatives and friends stated that there was no record of any heart issues in his past. Just this fact alone aroused inquiries and raised eyebrows. No autopsy was performed despite the unusual timing and the absence of a medical history. This omission only fueled speculation and gave birth to numerous theories regarding his death's true cause.

According to some of Monast's associates, he was harassed and intimidated in the days leading up to his death, adding to the suspicion that something sinister was at work. Because of how quickly after his arrest Serge Monast passed away, many people who admired his work saw him as a martyr.

The events surrounding Serge Monast's detention and death are still discussed today. Project Blue Beam in particular continues to have an impact, and there are still unanswered issues about Monast's untimely passing.

THE QUEST FOR TRUTH

The quest for truth can be complex and it can challenge our perceptions, but we should never shy away from it. Whether true or not, Project Blue Beam serves as a lesson for our day. It makes us pause and consider whether we could still have faith in a world full of delusions and doubts. In the midst of all the noise, how can we recognize God's voice? The apostle Paul's words, as he spoke about our need to grow up in Christ, ring with timeless insight:

> *So that we may no longer be children, tossed to and fro by the waves and carried about by every wind of doctrine, by human cunning, by craftiness in deceitful schemes. Rather, speaking the truth in love, we are to grow up in every way into him who is the head, into Christ* (Ephesians 4:14-15 ESV).

THE CALL TO ACTION

There is a call to action beneath all the mystery and uncertainty. It is our duty as believers to interact with the world in a thoughtful, wise, and compassionate manner with discernment. This story causes us to think and provokes us to question human authority.

According to C.S. Lewis, "Christianity is a statement which, if false, is of no importance, and if true, of infinite importance. The one thing it cannot be is moderately important."[33]

The story of Project Blue Beam, whether it is a historical curiosity or a metaphor for something else, serves as a springboard for deeper research. We must not trust what we hear or see. We must trust the Word of God.

CHAPTER ELEVEN

THE SONS OF GOD

From AI to aliens, we have seen how satan can easily influence a society. His web of deception spreads across all of man's fallen history—but our God is greater. What distinguishes our God from all other false gods? In the first place, He is the *only* God. He is not simply the most powerful deity in all creation. He is also the most holy and unique being there ever was or will be. I want us to look at the different beings in God's created universe, but I want you to always remember that He is God, and beside Him there is no other.

By understanding the nature of the different beings in His created order, we might better understand our role in creation and the authority in which He has called us to walk.

He created the heavens and the earth. He is the author of life and the architect of our redemption, whereby our Redeemer, Christ, the Son of God, was:

> Declared to be the **Son of God** with power, according to
> the spirit of holiness, by the resurrection from the dead
> (Romans 1:4 KJV).

Through the power of the resurrection, Christ was reborn as the firstborn Son of God—being the first so that many more could follow:

> *For whom he did foreknow, he also did predestinate*
> *to be conformed to the image of his Son, that he might*
> *be the firstborn among many brethren* (Romans 8:29
> KJV).

As children of God and joint heirs with Christ, we have an assured—and clearly defined—position in the kingdom as sons of God, as described in Romans 8:14-17 (KJV):

> *For as many as are led by the Spirit of God, they are*
> *the **sons of God**. For ye have not received the spirit of*
> *bondage again to fear; but ye have received the Spirit*
> *of adoption, whereby we cry, Abba, Father. The Spirit*
> *itself beareth witness with our spirit, that we are the*
> *children of God: and if children, then heirs; heirs of*
> *God, and joint-heirs with Christ.*

UNDERSTANDING THE SONS OF GOD: OLD AND NEW

We need to look first at the term *sons of God* in the Old Testament. It stands out as a central concept worthy of our attention. In the Hebrew text, *sons of God* is written as *b'nai Elohim*, a term with a great deal of significance and weight. According to Genesis 6:1-2, the "sons of God" mated with "the daughters of men," resulting in the birth of the Nephilim:

> *And it came to pass, when men began to multiply on*
> *the face of the earth, and daughters were born unto*
> *them, that the sons of God saw the daughters of men*

that they were fair; and they took them wives of all which they chose.

This is one of the Bible's most mysterious passages. This term appears to refer to supernatural entities that are distinct from humans and possess bizarre qualities. Looking more closely at the scriptures, we can ascertain at least a portion of their purpose:

> *Now there was a day when the **sons of God** came to present themselves before the Lord, and Satan came also among them* (Job 1:6 KJV).

The psalms also contain glimpses of these beings. In Psalm 89:6 (KJV), it is stated:

> *For who in the heaven can be compared unto the Lord? who among the **sons of the mighty** can be likened unto the Lord?*

This indicates that the "sons of the mighty" are no match for God, but they are viewed as beings with a great deal of power and splendor who are only inferior to the Most High God.

Moving into the New Testament use of the term *sons of God*, the meaning changes, primarily due to the Greek language and the social and cultural shifts of the age. In the Greek text, the phrase *sons of God* is often translated as *huioi Theou*, and its meaning expands. In Romans 8:14 (KJV), Paul writes:

> *For as many as are led by the Spirit of God, they are the **sons of God**.*

In the Old Testament, the term *sons of God* referred only to heavenly beings who were part of God's heavenly council, but in the New Testament, it includes those who have accepted Christ and are led by the Spirit. This represents a fundamental shift in understanding brought about by the birth, death, and resurrection of Jesus Christ, *the* Son of God. It elevates the potential status of all believers in Christ. Through Him, believers are adopted into the family of God, granted a parental relationship with the Most High, and given the right to be referred to as *sons of God.*

Does an understanding of the Nephilim shed light on our own adoption as sons of God? These spiritual entities mingled with humanity to create a hybrid race of giants. Now in the New Covenant, we are born again by the incorruptible seed of the Word of God and made new creatures in Christ Jesus. It's fascinating to consider the parallels.

The Book of Daniel is one of the most intriguing resources for understanding this subject. In Daniel 10, an angelic messenger is referred to as the prince of Persia. This being was not referred to as a *son of God*, but the context and language strongly indicate he belongs to the same order of beings mentioned in Genesis 6 and Job 1. Such a "prince" may have some influence over certain regions around the world.

What does this signify then? It may imply that a son of God, or "prince" in paradise, has responsibilities on earth. This brings us back to Genesis 6 and the Nephilim narrative. Not only were the nuptials between the sons of God and the daughters of men immoral, but they also disrupted the divine order and interfered with human affairs.

Cherubim and Seraphim

Cherubim and seraphim are mentioned frequently in the Bible, and their role as guardians is frequently highlighted. In the Garden of Eden, for instance, cherubim secure the path leading to the Tree of Life (see Genesis 3:24). In Isaiah 6, seraphim are discovered in God's throne chamber, proclaiming His holiness.

Watchers

The only place in the Bible where the word *watchers* appears is in Daniel 4. In Nebuchadnezzar's dream, these watchers predict that the monarch will be insane for a certain period of time. Even though they are not termed *sons of God*, their actions and behavior indicate that they have the same characteristics. It is conceivable to say that the watchers are the sons of God, or at least a subset of them, due to their ability to make and implement decisions and their apparent monitoring of what people do. This could provide additional insight into the roles these beings perform in the world.

THE ARCHANGELS CONTROVERSY

Michael, the archangel, is the only angel referred to by this label in the New Testament, which is found in Jude 1:9. This has sparked numerous debates regarding the existence of additional archangels. Gabriel is referred to as an archangel in Roman Catholic tradition, despite the fact that the New Testament does not explicitly state this. Seven archangels are mentioned in the Book of Enoch, but we will discuss its veracity later. Nevertheless, it is evident that archangels play a significant role in the spiritual realm, perhaps as leaders or commanders of God's celestial army.

Briefly, the biblical perspective on the different spiritual beings that God has created is not very straightforward. Each group of heavenly beings—sons of God, cherubim, seraphim, watchers, and archangels—serves a distinct purpose in God's plan. Even Paul the apostle says:

> *For we wrestle not against flesh and blood, but against principalities, against powers, against the rulers of the darkness of this world, against spiritual wickedness in high places* (Ephesians 6:12 KJV).

The ancient Greek translation of the Hebrew Bible, known as the Septuagint, had to determine how to convey Hebrew nuances in a foreign language. One of these issues was how to describe objects in the sky. In the Hebrew Bible, *Elohim* refers to gods, *ben Elohim* refers to sons of God. However, the Greek Septuagint frequently referred to all of these distinct individuals as *angelos* or angels.

Even though the word *angelos* does an excellent job of describing these beings as God's messengers or helpers, and is a divinely inspired translation, we can sometimes miss the subtleties in its reading. When we refer to all categories of celestial beings as angels, it can be difficult to distinguish between their various jobs, ranks, and roles. Mind you, this is not always a negative thing. On occasion, we can delve too deeply into the details of this issue and spin off into wild conspiracy theories. Understanding the subtle distinctions between these concepts is more than just a matter of academic rigor; it is also a matter of faithfully engaging with the Scriptures in order to appreciate the vast, complex celestial landscape that plays a critical part in God's unfolding eschatological plan.

To comprehend how important Christ's purpose is, we have to go back to God's original intent for creation, which was marred by rebellion. Christ's purpose in coming to earth was greater than we often realize. He came to restore order to a disordered universe. The life, death, and resurrection of Jesus inaugurated a new type of sonship. The apostle Paul writes:

> Because you are his sons, God sent the Spirit of his Son into our hearts, the Spirit who calls out, "Abba, Father" (Galatians 4:6 NIV).

This is a remarkable turn of events. Christ has elevated us to the status of sons of God, once reserved for the highest-ranking spirits. People are not only saved through Christ; they are also elevated, surpassing the unfaithful members of the first Divine Council mentioned in Job.

CONSEQUENCES FOR THE FUTURE

Even though this promotion has immediate effects, such as the fact that, as God's offspring, we can communicate with Him directly, it also contains astounding future promises. One of the most shocking is found in 1 Corinthians 6:3 (NKJV):

> Do you not know that we shall judge angels? How much more, things that pertain to this life?

This verse illustrates how Christ's work endeavors to radically alter the universe's order. Believers are intended to supplant unfaithful celestial beings, even to the extent of judging angels.

The implications are massive. At the conclusion of God's plan, it appears that the Divine Council will undergo a reorganization, with transformed and glorified faithful humans replacing disloyal and fallen ones. This new insight highlights the nature of the biblically described cosmic conflict: it is a struggle for the governance of creation itself, not just a war for individual souls.

Ultimately, when considering Christian eschatology, the concept of the sons of God is a crucial link between our knowledge of the past cosmic hierarchy and God's designs for a renewed and reordered future creation. Christ has made it possible for people to take on tasks and responsibilities that were unthinkable in the old world. When we consider how God's plan for the end of the world will unfold in the future, it becomes evident that the story of the sons of God is not merely an academic debate, but a living truth that strengthens our faith in Christ and His ultimate victory. This also shows why the antichrist will hide his face while we're on this planet.

WHY JESUS CAME TO EARTH

The incarnation, crucifixion, and resurrection are events that have universal ramifications echoing throughout the spiritual world. By understanding the fall of satan and the role of the sons of God, we can see Christ's mission in context. His advent is more than a plan B for repairing a broken human state; it is the focal point of a grand cosmic strategy to restore divine order and wholeness.

The roles of the sons of God, cherubim, seraphim, watchers, and even archangels demonstrate what was lost and what Christ came to restore. In Christ, a new type of son of God is born, one that is not limited to angels but encompasses all believers in Him.

A WORD OF CAUTION

This is just one theory, and it's important to remember that we still have much to learn. The majority of our celestial counterparts reside in a realm that we do not completely comprehend. So, as we continue to pursue information, stick close to the Word of God and you'll never go wrong.

Let's be like the Bereans, who were more honorable than the Thessalonians because they avidly listened to the Word and checked the Bible daily to ensure its accuracy (see Acts 17:11). With this perspective, we can study these intriguing topics in the fear of the Lord.

IS THERE A CONNECTION BETWEEN UFOS AND BIBLICAL EXTRATERRESTRIALS?

I've been asked a lot whether or not UFO sightings today could be linked to biblical accounts of extraterrestrial beings like the sons of God or the Nephilim.

We will discuss this in the next chapter. However, it must be made plain that the Bible does discuss heavenly beings but does not mention UFOs as we know them today (extraterrestrial physical life forms from another planet, operating advanced crafts). Nevertheless, it is not absurd to believe that there may be a connection. Numerous biblical accounts describe the appearance and movement of angels in ways that defy the laws of physics. For instance, Ezekiel saw wheels within wheels, and angels frequently radiate a brilliant splendor or ride flaming chariots. Could what many believe to be extraterrestrial activity actually be the spiritual world interacting with our physical world? Perhaps, but again we must exercise caution.

The central argument is that the Bible asserts that there are entities in the heavens with powers far beyond our comprehension. Even though UFOs remain largely unexplained, any potential links to the Bible's celestial hierarchy should be considered with prayer, critical thought, and in accordance with God's Word.

By asking such penetrating questions, we find ourselves at the crossroads of theology, apologetics, and cultural discourse. These discussions should always lead us back to Christ, who is *"the image of the invisible God, the firstborn over all creation"* (Colossians 1:15 NIV) and the answer to all of the mysteries of the universe.

Christ is at the center of God's plan to save the world, whether we're considering the vast cosmic order, theological semantics, or even modern mysteries like UFO sightings and alien abductions. These subjects are not strange from a religious standpoint. Instead, they help us learn more about the God we serve and the marvelous plan He has set in motion. As we stand on the brink of immortality, with one foot in this temporal world and the other in the eternal world, may we always seek to comprehend Him in all of His unfathomable complexity, majesty, and love.

CHAPTER TWELVE

THE EMERGENCE OF THE NEPHILIM

From the primordial days of Genesis to the prophetic revelations of Daniel and Revelation, you cannot help but encounter the Nephilim. Described as giants, fallen ones, or mighty men, these enigmatic characters loom like colossal shadows over the biblical landscape, leaving us to question who they were and what role they played in history. However, the most perplexing query is: could these same Nephilim have some connection to the antichrist and the end times? We've touched on this but let's revisit it and dive a little deeper.

GENESIS OF THE NEPHILIM

In the pre-diluvian world, recorded in the early chapters of the Book of Genesis, we have our first glimpse of what were later termed the Nephilim. Genesis 6:1-2 (NIV) states:

> *When human beings began to increase in number on the earth and daughters were born to them, the sons of God saw that the daughters of humans were beautiful, and they married any of them they chose.*

As we discussed in a previous chapter, some proposed that the sons of God were simply godly males from the line of Seth, while others more accurately suggest they were celestial beings—angels, who somehow were able to procreate with human women. The text itself alludes to something extraordinary by stating that the progeny of these unions were called the Nephilim: *"heroes of old, men of renown"* (Genesis 6:4 NIV).

What were the Nephilim precisely? The term *Nephilim* is frequently translated as "giants," and these entities were indeed described as unusually large and strong. However, the word derives from the Hebrew root *naphal*, which means "to fall." Could these beings be "the fallen ones"? There is no reason to believe that godly males from the line of Seth would produce a race of giants.

THE NEPHILIM AFTER THE FLOOD

If Genesis 6 leaves us with doubts, Numbers 13 intensifies the mystery. Here, horrified and disheartened Israelite spies return from an expedition into Canaan. Why?

> We saw the Nephilim there (the descendants of Anak come from the Nephilim). We seemed like grasshoppers in our own eyes, and we looked the same to them (Numbers 13:33 NIV).

Obviously, whatever the Nephilim were, they survived the flood or were reintroduced into the world afterword. This could have been done by more fallen angels engaging with the daughters of men or it could be that Noah's daughters-in-law carried those genes over into the new world.

The text introduces a new term—*Anakim*—who are described as being descended from the Nephilim. The Anakim were specifically localized Canaanite communities that were renowned for their size and strength. This association between the Anakim and the Nephilim adds another layer to the mystery, suggesting a continuity—or perhaps a recurrence—of these extraordinary beings, profoundly entrenched in the history of the biblical narrative.

OTHER BIBLICAL REFERENCES

As mentioned earlier, the Emim, Zamzummim, and Rephaim are mentioned in Deuteronomy 2:10-11, 20-21. Deuteronomy does not use the term "Nephilim," but it does introduce us to three communities that are similarly terrifying: the Emim, the Zamzummim, and the Rephaim. These nations are described as "a people strong and numerous, as tall as the Anakites" (see Deuteronomy 2). Later in the chapter, they are called *Rephaim*, but the Ammonites dubbed them *Zamzummim*.

The suggestion appears to be that these groups were additional Nephilim manifestations. Or perhaps they were distinct but similar; either way, the biblical narrative points to a recurring motif of large, powerful beings that exert a significant influence over God's people. They also possessed great technological advancements, which we'll discuss later.

FALLEN WARRIORS LIKE NEPHILIM

Ezekiel 32 is a dirge lamenting the city of Tyre's destruction, and it compares its slain warriors to the Nephilim. Despite the metaphorical nature of the reference, the connection between these mighty combatants and the mysterious Nephilim is striking. The verse in Ezekiel 32:27 (NIV) states:

> But they do not lie with the fallen warriors of old, who went down to the realm of the dead with their weapons of war—their swords placed under their heads and their shields resting on their bones—though these warriors also had terrorized the land of the living.

This association serves to emphasize the fear and power inspired by these entities. Whether literal or figurative, the Nephilim and related groups are consistently portrayed as extraordinary and terrifying beings. While none of these passages definitively clarify the Nephilim's nature or identity, they add to the complexity of this fascinating topic.

THE WATCHERS AND THEIR OFFSPRING IN THE BOOK OF ENOCH

Although the Book of Enoch is not part of the canonical Scriptures, it does provide a detailed account of the Nephilim. This archaic text delves deeply into the wayward angels who mated with human women to produce the race of giants. The narrative portrays a vivid picture of their skills, influence, and ultimate judgment.

Nonetheless, it is essential to consider the Book of Enoch with skepticism. The text is excluded from the canon of Scripture for a variety of theological and historical reasons, which we will examine in greater detail. Therefore, despite the fact that the Book of Enoch is intriguing and provides a more detailed account of these mysterious entities, its veracity and applicability to Christian doctrine are debatable.

WHAT ABOUT THE BOOK OF ENOCH?

A subject as convoluted and mysterious as the Book of Enoch can be as hard to untangle as an ancient serpent. The Book of Enoch isn't just any ordinary document; it's classified as "pseudepigrapha," which means it's professing to be something it's not. "Why exactly is this a pseudepigrapha, and why should I care?" It's a valid question. The term refers to writings that falsely claim to be the work of a biblical figure, in this case Enoch. The label casts a shadow over the text, a shadow that dates back hundreds of years.

How does the Christian community as a whole view the Book of Enoch, and why is it deemed significant to investigate? It obviously appeals to our innate curiosity and our ceaseless desire for something *new*.

The renowned Dead Sea Scrolls include six fragments of the Book of Enoch dating back to approximately 300 B.C. The discovery of these artifacts offers a rare glimpse into a long-lost era. This is where we can all agree that the Book of Enoch has value. However, even in the first century, this book was the topic of passionate debate. Some thought this book had merit while others, such as Origen and Jerome, did not recognize its value.[34]

As fascinating as this book may be, we must be cautious. How we approach it could determine how we view the inspiration of scripture in the future. One of the greatest battles of the next decade will be over the infallibility of the Word of God. If we become too loosy-goosey in our understanding of this subject, we may open the door to something far more damaging than we could have imagined. The Book of Enoch is a fascinating historical curiosity, but should it be trusted? We must be like the Bereans in Acts 17, who daily examined the Scriptures to confirm the apostles' message.

ABSENCE IN THE HEBREW BIBLE AND JESUS' TEACHINGS

The Book of Enoch deserves a healthy dose of suspicion. There is no mention of the Book of Enoch in the Old Testament. Why would this be the situation? The Old Testament prophets would have made reference to the book if it were a source of divine insight. When instructed to place the Word of God in the Ark of the Covenant, the Israelites placed the writings of Moses but not those of Enoch (which would have preceded Moses' writings).

Jesus, the personification of God's Word, encounters His disciples on the road to Emmaus and begins to explain the references to Himself in scripture. Notably, Jesus began with Moses instead (not Enoch):

> *Then He said to them, "O foolish ones, and slow of heart to believe in all that the prophets have spoken! Ought not the Christ to have suffered these things and to enter into His glory?" And beginning at Moses and all the Prophets, He expounded to them in all the Scriptures the things concerning Himself* (Luke 24:25-27 NKJV).

JUDE'S BIBLIOGRAPHY

Some suggest that Jude is quoting Enoch and that this alone should verify its importance. Non-biblical passages are frequently cited in the New Testament. Paul cited a worldly poet in Acts 17:28, and Titus did the same in Titus 1:12. Even if a biblical author cites a book, that provides no evidence that the book is inspired.

What was Jude referring to in Jude 1:14-15 (NIV)?

> *Enoch, the seventh from Adam, prophesied about them: "See, the Lord is coming with thousands upon thousands of his holy ones to judge everyone, and to convict all of them of all the ungodly acts they have committed in their ungodliness, and of all the defiant words ungodly sinners have spoken against him."*

Let's be careful not to read into the passage and hear something Jude is not saying. Jude alludes to a prophetic proclamation made by Enoch without citing a specific book. Moses did not specifically cite a book when he mentioned Adam and Eve in the Garden of Eden. He spoke under the guidance of the Holy Spirit. It is entirely conceivable that this is also how Jude obtained his information. Even if he cited a genuine book in circulation, this would not imply that he endorsed it. Jude could have also been referring to oral tradition passed down through the generations or an entirely different book. Alleged writings from Enoch come in many different forms and translations. We just don't know.

We do know that there are some strange things in those writings.

ERRORS IN ENOCH'S TEACHINGS

There are more questions than answers in the Book of Enoch. As we delve deeper into the teachings' substance, we find a minefield of contradictions and inaccuracies.

1. The command to offer sacrifices to the sun, moon, and stars can be found in Pseudo-Enoch 100:10-12. This is a radical departure from what the Bible teaches.

2. According to Pseudo-Enoch 67:1-3, angels constructed the Ark. However, the Bible makes it quite clear that Noah built it.

3. In Pseudo-Enoch 9:1-4, the author seems to endorse prayer to angels suggesting that the angels served as some kind of intercessory intermediaries. I don't need to tell you that we pray only to God, not to intermediaries in heaven.

4. Pseudo-Enoch also attempts to invoke sympathy for fallen angels (Pseudo-Enoch 13:1-7 and 15:1-2).

5. Pseudo-Enoch 69 goes on to attribute Eve's deception to an entity named "Gadreel" and not to satan.

6. Pseudo-Enoch 10:8-9 attributes the origin of human sin to an entity named Azazel. Where does satan fit into this?

7. First Enoch 7:2 claims that the giants were 3,000 cubits tall (4,500 feet or 0.86 miles; conservative estimates are 450 feet).

These fallacies in the Book of Enoch contradict biblical doctrine and introduce ambiguity where clarity should exist. Proceed with caution when exploring the Book of Enoch, recognizing its cultural and historical value while rejecting its doctrinal inconsistencies. The ultimate foundation of our faith must be the Word of God, not the shifting sediments of human legends.

When asked about this book, I often reply with two key questions:

1. What scriptural evidence do we have that this is true?

2. What practical difference does it make in the average Christian's life?

I often resort to these two questions when exploring a variety of contentious topics, such as the nature of the Nephilim or the genesis of demons.

The Book of Enoch provides an enthralling glimpse into the thoughts and worldviews of centuries past through its vivid legends and fantastical stories. The Book of Enoch is a literary work as opposed to an authoritative text. Yes, we can certainly learn from it. We can see how individuals struggled with spiritual truths and attempted to fathom their surroundings. Nonetheless, we must always maintain perspective and recognize the distinction between human speculation and divine revelation.

This is a question of both spiritual and theological precision. If non-canonical writings like the Book of Enoch were elevated to the status of authoritative scripture, our entire faith would be compromised. Therefore, let us approach the Book of Enoch with historical and theological foresight. Accept it for what it is, but never elevate it to a position of authority. The Bible must be the basis for our faith, hope, and manner of life. We find our firm foundation there. There, we discover our absolute truth. Our faith and confidence in God are grounded in the Bible.

Always remember that everything you need to know about any biblical subject or character can be found in the Bible itself. Everything you need to know about Enoch is in the Bible.

THE BOOK OF GIANTS

The Book of Giants, which has survived in fragments and is considered to be part of the Manichaean canon, is another text worthy of mention. This text also explores the legends surrounding giants and their interactions with humans. Similar to the Book of Enoch, the Book of Giants depicts these beings as having a significant impact on human history by imparting forbidden knowledge and perpetrating a multitude of transgressions.

Again, be cautious about considering these accounts as authoritative or doctrinally sound. They are not. They can, however, provide cultural context and perhaps even some historical background, but they do not and must not carry the same weight as the Bible in shaping our theological perspectives. These documents do not enjoy the same level of credibility as the canonical books of the Bible.

THE NEPHILIM
AND THE END OF THE AGE

One of the most interesting passages in the Bible concerning the Nephilim in an eschatological context is Daniel 2:43 (ESV), which states:

As you saw the iron mixed with soft clay, so they will mix with one another in marriage, but they will not hold together, just as iron does not mix with clay.

Even though we've discussed this in a previous chapter, it bears repeating that some theologians and scholars have speculated that the phrase "they will mingle with the offspring of men" could signify the return of the Nephilim or something similar in the end times. If, as Genesis 6 suggests, these beings were once able to interbreed with humans, is it possible that a comparable interbreeding could occur in the future, particularly during pivotal eschatological events? Others suggest that like Nimrod of old, transhumanism and the rise of AI will be the ultimate meaning behind this iron and clay depicted in his dream.

THE BEAST AND THE NEPHILIM IN REVELATION 13

Revelation 13 introduces us to the Beast, a figure that has been the subject of much theological speculation. Some have even suggested that the Beast may be a Nephilim or share some characteristics with these mysterious entities. This is strictly speculative, but it opens the door to a fascinating conversation about the nature of evil forces active in the end times. If the Nephilim were in some way disruptive to God's order in the past, could a similar being reappear in the end times? Does Daniel indicate that the antichrist will be in this Nephilim class?

THE MAN OF LAWLESSNESS

In his second letter to the Thessalonians, the apostle Paul describes "the man of lawlessness" as one who opposes and exalts himself above every deity or object of worship. While the identity of this enigmatic figure has been widely debated, the notion that he could be a Nephilim is a hypothesis worth considering. The extraordinary abilities, deception potential, and powerful impact on humanity that characterized the Nephilim could conceivably be reflected in this "man of lawlessness," particularly given his seemingly supernatural characteristics.

In each of these instances, we proceed with caution, mindful that speculation can easily outpace biblical evidence. There is a delicate line between speculation and interpretation when discussing the Nephilim and their possible eschatological return. Given the limited information found in the Bible, it is essential that any hypotheses or doctrinal positions be firmly rooted in biblical exegesis and theological rigor. Unchecked speculation can devolve into sensationalism, clouding our comprehension of more fundamental biblical truths and detracting from the central message of the Gospel.

What theological implications arise from contemplating the antichrist as a potential Nephilim? We are commanded in the Bible to not be ignorant concerning the enemy's devices. The antichrist spirit is already at work in the earth, and understanding these things can help us to see through his plan.

This also raises questions in the minds of some about the extent or limits of redemption: is the antichrist beyond redemption in a manner that surpasses the wickedness of ordinary humans? Does this change our understanding of the "unpardonable sin"? Some suggest that the antichrist's transhumanist agenda will alter the DNA of those who receive his mark, making them irredeemable. I'm not convinced.

The mark is a reward for worshipping the beast. This act is what is irredeemable.

WHY HIDE IT? GIANTS IN HISTORICAL PERSPECTIVE

To make this chapter complete we need to revisit what we've said about giants throughout history as well. Why has the existence of these giants been hidden by the world? From the mythological tales of ancient civilizations to the epic sagas recounted around medieval campfires, the concept of giants has been a subject of universal fascination that transcends cultures and periods. This intrigue is not limited to folklore and legend; it has also pervaded scientific and theological discourse. Whether it's the titans of Greek mythology or the biblical accounts of the Nephilim, the notion that beings of immense size and strength once roamed the Earth has a firm hold on the human imagination.

If this has been so pervasive throughout our history, why has it been hidden for the last century? Could it be that the enemy is attempting to whitewash the historical record? Is there a deliberate attempt to remove anything from our past that will restore our sense of wonder or faith in God?

HISTORICAL ACCOUNTS NOT FOUND IN THE BIBLE

In contrast to sacred texts, history has not remained mute on the topic of giants. Turning our attention to historical texts and accounts that mention giants, let's see what the past has for us.

Abraham Lincoln's Address at Niagara Falls

Abraham Lincoln, the 16th president of the United States, is an often-overlooked historical example who lends gravitas to this conversation about giants. In the speech he delivered in 1848 at Niagara Falls, Lincoln pondered the notion that the waters had witnessed the passage of time and possibly the presence of giants. He stated:

> But still there is more. It calls up the indefinite part. When Columbus first sought this continent—when Christ suffered on the Cross—when Moses led Israel through the Red Sea—nay even when Adam first came from the hand of his Maker—then as now, Niagara was roaring here. The eyes of that species of extinct giants whose bones fill the Mounds of America, have gazed on Niagara as ours do now. Contemporary with the whole race of men, and older than the first man Niagara is as strong and fresh today as ten thousand years ago.[35]

Additional Historical Texts

The Greeks spoke of titans, and the Norse sagas frequently describe battles with enormously powerful entities. In Eastern traditions, there are also accounts of monstrous beings resembling humans but possessing extraordinary physical and sometimes supernatural abilities.

The significance of these accounts lies not only in their fantastical elements, but also in the recurring themes and similarities they share, despite being frequently separated by geographical borders and eras. These reoccurring elements imply a uniformity of understanding woven through time, allowing us to ponder whether these beings were not merely figments of someone's imagination, but perhaps once coexisted with us on Earth.

While we should be cautious about claiming historical accounts as definitive proof of the existence of giants, the pervasiveness of these tales in cultures around the world should give us pause.

ARCHAEOLOGICAL DISCOVERIES

Archaeology provides us with a tantalizing, albeit controversial, corpus of evidence. Throughout the years, excavations and discoveries have unearthed skeletal remains and artifacts indicating the existence of unusually large human-like entities. Despite the fact that the veracity of some of these findings is frequently contested, they provide enticing data. Tales of giant skulls with horns and even two rows of teeth are not uncommon.

The Lovelock Cave Findings

On a more substantive note, Lovelock Cave in Nevada offers a compelling collection of artifacts and skeletal remains. The cave yielded thousands of artifacts, including the remains of enormous human-like skeletons, when it was discovered in the early 20th century. The oral traditions of the Paiute Native American tribes speak of cannibalistic, red-haired monsters who terrorized the land. Despite the fact that mainstream archaeology generally rejects the idea that these remains belonged to beings substantially larger than modern humans, the findings have sparked considerable debate.

Some have speculated that the skeletal remains and unique artifacts discovered in Lovelock Cave could be evidence of a race of giants, providing support for the numerous stories and legends that span cultures and millennia. The scientific community remains divided on the implications of the Lovelock Cave discoveries, but they undoubtedly add a layer of complexity to our understanding of the types of beings that may have walked the Earth before humans.

Archaeological evidence is frequently open to interpretation, but it provides us with intriguing avenues of investigation. The objective is to approach these discoveries with a healthy dose of skepticism and an openness to the grander possibilities they imply.

The Smithsonian Controversy

The alleged role of the Smithsonian Institution in concealing evidence is one of the most persistent and contentious narratives in the discourse surrounding the existence of giants. This esteemed American institution whose stated purpose is "the increase and diffusion of knowledge" has been accused of concealing or destroying artifacts and skeletal remains that point to the existence of giants, according to various claims.

Examining the Arguments

The sources of these allegations vary from amateur historians to fringe scientists, and they are frequently disseminated in books and online forums that take a critical or conspiratorial stance toward mainstream archaeology. In lieu of evidence, these claims frequently rely on anecdotal accounts, such as tales of giant skeletons being transported to the Smithsonian, never to be displayed or mentioned again.

While it is essential to scrutinize any institution with significant cultural influence, the absence of evidence renders these claims at best dubious. There are no verifiable internal documents, credible internal whistleblowers, or credible external audits to support these allegations. In addition, the Smithsonian has made extensive archives and catalogues available to the public, and none of them contain such controversial items. Of course, the absence of these findings from their archives does not preclude their existence.

A Balanced Point of View

While remaining receptive to new evidence, it is essential to approach such broad assertions with a balanced viewpoint. Extraordinary claims require extraordinary evidence, a maxim that is especially applicable when the integrity of a long-standing scientific institution is in question.

The Smithsonian controversy serves as a poignant reminder of the complex interplay between public trust and institutional authority. Skepticism is a healthy component of academic and theological inquiry, but it must be coupled with intellectual integrity. In our search for understanding in the labyrinthine world of giants—biblical or otherwise—a balanced, evidence-based approach will serve us best. All of that being said, neither the Smithsonian nor any other institution can serve as our final authority.

The Bible is the most accurate history book that has ever been or will be. It is unique in that it is the only book that records history in advance. Let's look at what it has to say about our future.

CHAPTER THIRTEEN

THE ANTICHRIST SPIRIT

In the past, a well-worn strategy of preachers trying to attract attention and crowds would be to preach about the antichrist. The specter of an enigmatic world leader who would first use flatteries and finally resort to force to contain and coerce the masses has been the pulp for countless sermons in years past. It is not my intention to repeat the spectacular pronouncements of end-time preachers of years gone by. I will remind you that every generation has claimed the distinction of producing the person who would become the antichrist. An antichrist has existed in every century and yet one by one, all of these candidates were ushered out of history by death.

However, we cannot ignore the plain language of the Bible that affirms there will indeed be an ungodly leader who comes on the world stage and swears he has the answers to humankind's most pressing problems. The only price necessary to participate in his magnanimity will be to give him unquestioning allegiance. Much of the world will be more than willing to do so, regardless of the risks involved. As I intend to show, the antichrist and AI are made for each other. In fact, it is entirely probable that the antichrist's reign could not be possible without the technological benefits of AI gone wrong.

I believe that this is a subject whose time has come. There are those in the Church who object to any teaching regarding the antichrist.

They say, "I'm looking for *the* Christ, not the antichrist." While it is true that we need to remain focused on Jesus Christ and not the antichrist, Christians must have a sound grasp on biblical eschatology, and that includes a proper understanding of the ultimate impostor who will appear near the end of this age of human history.

Others say, "What has that got to do with what people are dealing with every single day of their lives? People are struggling, and they need encouragement." You can be discouraged and still go to heaven, but you cannot fall prey to the antichrist spirit and still get to heaven. Yes, many are struggling, and many are discouraged, and there is much in the Bible that will help them with struggles and discouragement. But to ignore the reality of the antichrist spirit that is already in the world is to leave people vulnerable to disillusionment and deception.

When you consider the issues we face individually, as well as those that we face as a nation, you will come to no other conclusion than they are connected to the antichrist spirit and a systematic preparation for his arrival. In fact, there are those who will maintain that world conditions are not getting worse but are actually getting better. When someone takes this position, they usually cite metrics that have to do with physical or material conditions to back up their belief.

However, we must get the mind of God on this subject. When God looks at a generation, how does He decide whether it is getting better or getting worse? Does He look at their standard of living? Does God decide whether a generation is doing better by the technological advancements they possess? Does He look at the length of a person's life or their quality of life? What are the standards by which God determines if things are getting better or not?

We have examples that answer this question from the Old Testament. Before the flood, the Bible says the hearts of men became evil *continually* (see Genesis 6:5). Before the overthrow of Sodom and Gomorrah, God Himself came to the city to see whether the reports He heard of degradation and debauchery were true. You can read about it in Genesis 19.

What has historically caused catastrophic divine judgment to fall upon a city, a region, or a generation? It is tempting to blame men's evil thoughts and evil actions. However, that is not the whole story. Men have had evil thoughts and evil actions since the fall in Genesis 3. I believe the factor that prompted God's judgment was the *frequency* of evil thoughts and evil actions. They became not just random, but continuous. It was not that evil was punctuated or interrupted by good; evil was continuous and unbroken. The image of God and the consciousness of anything that was holy was extinguished by men's choice to pursue sin. The only solution was judgment.

If other generations could not escape the judgment of God, what about this generation? Look at the technological advancements that we have today. Have they improved the frequency of righteous thoughts or of evil thoughts? I would submit to you that today, more than any other time in history, men and women, even those who are righteous, have greater opportunity to think evil thoughts. The reason is that they have a device in their pockets, or in their hands, that keeps wickedness within reach at all times.

Is the world getting better or is it getting worse? People will give you different answers depending on their worldview. However, from God's perspective, things are quickly decaying and spiraling out of control. The world is ready for an antichrist figure to come upon the scene.

HIS RISE TO POWER

How is it that thinking people will accept the leadership of a person who may not have their best interests in mind? Consider the example of ancient Israel. They were threatened by the Philistines, and they decided they had to have a king to lead them. God did not want them to have a king, but they insisted, and God gave them their desire. King Saul was a disappointment in more ways than one, but his elevation to kingship points out people's willingness to accept and even desire something that is ultimately not good for them.

Paul-Henri Spaak, a prominent diplomat of a previous generation was credited with this quote: "What we want is a man of sufficient stature to hold the alliances of all people and to lift us out of the economic morass into which we are sinking. Send us such a man, be he god or devil, we will receive him." Such thinking emphasizes temporal gain without regard to eternal pain. Unfortunately, it appears that this point of view is gaining acceptance in the world. The world is being prepared for the antichrist.

The prophet Samuel minced no words when he told Israel what would happen when they had a king. You can read his warnings in 1 Samuel 8. John does the same thing in describing the antichrist. If you want him (or even if you don't), this is what is in store for you:

> *And I stood upon the sand of the sea, and saw a beast rise up out of the sea, having seven heads and ten horns, and upon his horns ten crowns, and upon his heads the name of blasphemy. And the beast which I saw was like unto a leopard, and his feet were as the feet of a bear, and his mouth as the mouth of a lion: and the dragon gave him his power, and his seat, and great authority. And I saw one of his heads as it were*

wounded to death; and his deadly wound was healed: and all the world wondered after the beast.

And they worshipped the dragon which gave power unto the beast: and they worshipped the beast, saying, Who is like unto the beast? who is able to make war with him? And there was given unto him a mouth speaking great things and blasphemies: and power was given unto him to continue forty and two months. And he opened his mouth in blasphemy against God, to blaspheme his name, and his tabernacle, and them that dwell in heaven. And it was given unto him to make war with the saints, and to overcome them: and power was given him over all kindreds, and tongues, and nations. And all that dwell upon the earth shall worship him, whose names are not written in the book of life of the Lamb slain from the foundation of the world. If any man have an ear, let him hear (Revelation 13:1-9 KJV).

SIGNS OF THE ANTICHRIST

There are more than one hundred passages in Scripture that describe the antichrist. There are less than fifty about Adam. Again and again, God gives explicit details about who this man of mystery is—without, of course, identifying him by name. His characteristics, his intention, and his agenda are obvious, but much of the Church, like an ostrich, sticks its head in the sand and tries to ignore the eventuality of his appearing. I don't say this to scare you, but to prepare you. I don't want to make you anxious, but I want to make you aware. We must watch and pray. Being prepared, being aware, watching and praying will bring us the peace and hope that God has for us individually and for the Church as a whole. John, from his first letter, says it this way:

> *Beloved, believe not every spirit, but try the spirits whether they are of God: because many false prophets are gone out into the world. Hereby know ye the Spirit of God: Every spirit that confesseth that Jesus Christ is come in the flesh is of God: and every spirit that confesseth not that Jesus Christ is come in the flesh is not of God: and this is that spirit of antichrist, whereof ye have heard that it should come; and even now already is it in the world. Ye are of God, little children, and have overcome them: because greater is he that is in you, than he that is in the world* (1 John 4:1-3 KJV).

The Church has often assumed that the *he* John is referring to is the devil, but that is not entirely correct. The *he* John has in mind is the *spirit of antichrist*. Understand that there is a man who is coming who will be possessed by the devil, a master of the occult—indeed, of all the satanic arts. He may be an atheist, an agnostic, or what is more likely, he may act as though he is a deeply religious person. (He undoubtedly will be, but not in the manner that most people think of religion.)

- He will be quick to pervert everything that comes under his influence.
- He will be involved in every sin imaginable while acting like a model citizen.
- He will deceive many.

That man is coming, but before he appears, John tells us very plainly that the antichrist spirit *"is already in the world."* John also gives us some specific markers by which we can identify that spirit.

- It will deny that Jesus came in the flesh by means of the virgin birth.
- It will deny the relationship between Jesus and the Father.
- It will deny the reality of the Trinity.
- It will deny that Jesus is God.

You may be wondering how people can give any measure of credibility to a person who pretends to be religious yet who denies what seem to be obvious truths about God. How is it possible that he wins the unstinting allegiance of multitudes when what he is advocating is so blatantly false?

One reason is that so many, even among those who claim to be believers, are unfamiliar with basic Bible doctrines. They are strangers to the Bible themselves, and can we blame them? They never heard the truths of the Word of God from the pulpit either because the preacher was preoccupied with *more important issues* or he was terrified to touch on it himself.

People are becoming numb to Gospel Truth. They have heard so many diverging arguments regarding God or the Bible on social media that they essentially have stopped listening. When someone comes along and presents them with a candy-coated gospel while offering to drink a beer or smoke weed with them, they are ready to get on board regardless of what the leader is saying, and no matter how outrageous it may seem.

Another reason for the success of the antichrist's advent is his skillful and selective use of propaganda as a tool of persuasion. Do you think social media outlets have become adept at manipulating data to promote certain narratives and discredit others? Wait until the antichrist harnesses the power of advanced AI capabilities to control what you hear. He will make all past and current efforts at media manipulation look like child's play.

THE HERALD OF THE ANTICHRIST'S COMING

Perhaps the greatest factor that leads to the antichrist's acceptance is the spirit of antichrist that is preparing the way for him. John the Baptist was the herald of Christ's coming. The antichrist will also have a clever and capable master of information manipulation who will twist his lies into a semblance of the truth. This character is identified as the false prophet in Revelation 19:20. He will make Joseph Goebbels, Valenti Beria, and Mao's misinformation minions look like rank amateurs in comparison. The worldview he will sell people is socialism. It will not be a difficult task for many, since they have already succumbed to the siren song of socialist doctrine. They will need little persuasion since what the antichrist will offer them is something they have already bought into. They don't realize that it is a deal with the devil, and their part of the wager is their eternal soul.

Please don't think that I am saying that because socialism will be a major factor in preparing the way for the antichrist's advent that capitalism is the only economic system that is of God. God's ways are not man's ways. What God has in mind for the earth is neither capitalism nor socialism, but an economic system designed by the One who created it and ultimately owns it all.

What I am saying is that socialism has a fundamental flaw that makes it unworkable when it comes to equal outcomes for human beings. It is this: a foundational premise of socialism is that man is essentially good. The only things that are blocking man's continuing quest for perfection are inequities in the human condition caused by the lust for money and power. All men need to do to experience perfection is to give all their money and power to the state, so that the state can distribute resources equitably to all.

When anyone has the temerity to remind the current crop of socialists that their preferred worldview has a terrible track record of mayhem, disaster, and blood, they are undaunted in their quest for utopia. They claim that the benighted despots of the past did not have the advantages available to us in the 21st century. Now, they say, we can do socialism the way it is supposed to be done, and success will be inevitable. In the meantime, if a few million people die, that is a small price to pay for saving the planet. They maintain that there are too many *useless eaters* anyway. This is the current position of the World Economic Forum and its false prophet, Yuval Noah Harari. They are maneuvering to take hold of the levers of power, and America's leaders seem to be falling in line.

I understand that there is more to socialist doctrine than this, but I am emphasizing the aspect of socialism that requires men to believe that they are basically good and capable of perfection as a result of their own effort. This is a lie that is conclusively refuted by the testimony of human history, the clear record of the Bible, and the perfect plan of redemption.

This idea of men achieving perfection by submission to the all-powerful, benevolent state qualifies socialism to be a main tenet of the antichrist's doctrine, since he will seek to control the apparatus of power, and he will eventually become the personification of the state. If people are already conditioned to submit to the state, that will make his job much easier, since less persuasion or coercion will be required for them to give their allegiance to him.

Socialist doctrines and dogma are advancing all around us. It seems that every day's headlines bring us another outrageous proposal or policy that would have been laughed to scorn or mercilessly mocked a generation or even a decade ago. Now they seem to be standard operating procedure in many places. This is not a right or left issue or a matter of adherence to a political party. The conflict goes much deeper than that. It involves an ongoing and intensifying battle for the souls of men.

The antichrist spirit is better known for what it denies than for what it advocates. As I mentioned earlier, this spirit will deny the virgin birth, which we must believe to be saved. It denies the relationship between the Father and Jesus, as well as the person of the Holy Spirit, attacking the Trinity as an unworkable concept, since it cannot be understood by the rational mind. It will deny that Jesus is God. The antichrist spirit may give Jesus credit for being a good man or a prophet, but it denies Him as the only substitute for the sin of man. The antichrist spirit loves religion but has a problem with Jesus Christ. Remember, this spirit wants to either remove Jesus or replace Jesus.

This is what Paul was talking about in 1 Corinthians 15. He writes of fighting a wild beast at Ephesus. He was never thrown into an arena where he fought actual beasts. He was referring to the antichrist spirit. He said he fought the beast in Ephesus, and there he saw a mighty revival.

Today, you are fighting the beast in your daily life. You feel the pressure and the stress on your family, in your finances, in your relationships, and in your ability to witness your faith. In addition to all the natural circumstances that come against you, there is an antichrist spirit that opposes your efforts to succeed in fulfilling your God-given purpose.

Second Thessalonians was written by the great apostle Paul to the church of Thessalonica. The occasion of his letter to them was that he got word that they had received a letter as though it was written by him. Someone had forged a letter, signed it from Paul, and sent it to them. (Having an account hacked is not a recent phenomenon.) The letter told them, among other things, that they had missed the blessed hope and catching away of the saints. He wrote to reassure them and to remind them of what he had told them when he was personally present with them. The Book of 2 Thessalonians also contains an urgent emphasis on the last days, and it warned the Church to beware of those who had doctrines different from Paul's on that subject. Here is one important passage:

> Now we beseech you, brethren, by the coming of our Lord Jesus Christ, and by our gathering together unto him. That ye be not soon shaken in mind, or be troubled, neither by spirit, nor by word, nor by letter as from us, as that the day of Christ is at hand. Let no man deceive you by any means: for that day shall not come, except there come a falling away first, and that man of sin be revealed, the son of perdition; Who opposeth and exalteth himself above all that is called God, or that is worshipped; so that he as God sitteth in the temple of God, shewing himself that he is God.
>
> Remember ye not, that, when I was yet with you, I told you these things? And now ye know what withholdeth that he might be revealed in his time. For the mystery of iniquity doth already work: only he who now letteth will let, until he be taken out of the way. And then shall that Wicked be revealed, whom the Lord shall consume with the spirit of his mouth, and shall destroy with the

brightness of his coming: Even him, whose coming is after the working of Satan with all power and signs and lying wonders (2 Thessalonians 2:1-9 KJV).

The apostle Paul shows us that the antichrist is constantly trying to emerge on the world scene. However, there is a restraining force that is hindering the antichrist from being revealed and taking his place of power. That restraining force is the Holy Ghost-filled, fire-baptized Church of Jesus Christ. The Spirit of God within you is a restraining force holding back the plague, holding back the pestilence, holding back the depression, holding back the divorce, holding back the complete collapse of the economy, and so much more. You are the restrainer through the power of the Holy Spirit. You are pushing back against the antichrist spirit—and no weapon formed against you will prosper.

The only antidote to the spirit of antichrist is the real Christ within you, who is the hope of glory. Through the Spirit of God, you are empowered to proclaim the truth of the Gospel of Jesus Christ everywhere you go. Your influence in your family, your home, your community, and your workplace are all impediments that make it impossible for the antichrist to enact his agenda as long as you are on the earth. You are still here, and that is why he is not here—yet.

You are the antichrist's worst nightmare!

CHAPTER FOURTEEN

THE ANTICHRIST AGENDA

There are different names given to the antichrist in Scripture, all of which reveal some aspect of his nature and character. He is called the man of sin, the son of perdition, the wicked one, the prince that shall come, the little horn, the king of Babylon, and the beast. All of these point to the same character—the antichrist. *Anti,* as used in his name, comes from the Greek word which means *against* or *in place of.* This spirit of opposition, embodied in a man, will seek to either exclude or replace the Messiah, the Lord Jesus Christ. A few of the more notable characteristics of the antichrist are:

- He will gain power through political intrigue.
- He will help solidify a one-world government and a one-world currency.
- He will work with an ecumenical religious system (at least for the first half of his reign).
- He will make socialism the root of his governmental structure.
- He will deceive many by means of miraculous signs and wonders.
- He will have a contagious desire for sin and lawlessness.

- He will have an unquenchable appetite to persecute anyone who does not submit to him.

- He will have a particular and perfect hatred for the Jews.

- He will create a culture of harassment, intimidation, and persecution that will weary and wear out all who oppose any of his policies or plans.

This man of sin can be identified, according to Revelation 13:18 (KJV): "*his number is Six hundred threescore and six*." In the antichrist, we will see man's carnal nature reaching its apex. We do not know what the number associated with his name means. What we do know is that six, the number of man, tripled, gets as close to the number seven as possible without mimicking it exactly. It seems to represent the greatest example of man trying to become God.

Revelation 13 reveals another beast, in addition to the first one. This is the false prophet, the propagandist extraordinaire of the antichrist's reign. I find it interesting that the second beast has the form of a lamb—which is also a counterfeit of the Lamb of God, our Redeemer. This false lamb has two horns, the meaning of which has been the subject of endless speculation. Horns in this context often refer to power, dominion, authority, or kingdoms. If that is the case here, the two horns represent two seats of authority. Could it be that these two horns represent two religious systems? If so, which ones could they possibly be?

Here is a radical suggestion that may help resolve some seeming inconsistencies and reconcile some impossibilities. What if these two horns represent Christianity and Islam? The Christianity that would be involved by the time of the antichrist's advent would not be the same Christian faith that you or I know now. It would be a horribly mutated form of traditional orthodox Christianity that would be nothing but a mockery of its current iteration. In the event this indeed becomes a reality, it should not come as a surprise. Certain cults have already co-opted the language and symbolism of traditional Christianity while perverting the faith once delivered to the saints into an unholy and unrecognizable form. What is more, some current mainline denominations have morphed into a toxic mixture of Christianity and other belief systems, accepting and even celebrating behaviors and practices that have historically been soundly condemned by the Bible and traditional Christian doctrine. The practice of calling something Christianity that is not Christianity has abundant precedent.

In addition, some misguided individuals have already tried to mix Christianity with Islam—a so-called *Chrislam*, if you will. This is an effort to reconcile the fundamental differences between the two religions and allow their respective adherents to accept one another— or at least tolerate one another. The impulse to mix religions has a name—it is called syncretism, and it has been going on ever since religions began.

Let me take this a step further. What if this ungodly amalgamation is not Christianity and Islam, but Judaism and Islam? Before you dismiss this as a crackpot theory, keep in mind that whatever religious system is touched by the antichrist's influence will be distorted into a form that is essentially unrecognizable compared to their current belief systems. There are a few superficial similarities between Judaism and Islam. Both religions trace their origins to Abraham—Jews through Isaac, and Muslims through Ishmael. Both of them regard themselves as people of a book—Jews have their Tanakh, and Muslims their Koran. Neither of them regard Jesus as the Son of God.

What if some charismatic world leader was able, beyond all fragments of hope, to forge a consensus between these religions, causing them to agree about some fundamental concepts that would lead to peace between them? He would be hailed as a diplomat and negotiator without equal. He would be vaulted to prominence and prestige beyond any of his predecessors or peers. Many nations of the world would look to him as the solution to their problems.

He would (reluctantly, as a show of false humility) accept their offer to appoint him as a leader without any limitations or restrictions. They would obey his word as law and cater to his every whim. Such a leader would be able to craft an agreement that would end the historic conflicts between Muslims and Jews and would enable the Jewish temple to be rebuilt on Temple Mount in Jerusalem. He would fashion a treaty with Israel that would guarantee its security and sovereignty. All of this would happen during the first three and a half years of his advent, while he was relentlessly positioning and promoting himself as a man of peace, rational thinking, and unselfish beneficence.

DIVERSITY, EQUITY, AND INCLUSION

The antichrist will not make outrageous demands for people to worship him to the exclusion of all others when he first appears. He will come as a man of peace, a man of intellect, a man of science, a man of understanding—even a man of compassion and "tolerance." He will seduce entire nations into aligning themselves with him to advance his goals of Diversity, Equity, and Inclusion (DEI). They will have to forfeit their sovereignty, but what difference will national identities make when people's lives are at stake? It will all seem so reasonable.

Revelation 6 identifies several henchmen who will accompany the antichrist. They are war, famine, death, and hell. All these things will be benchmarks of his reign, but at first the antichrist will be the one who appears to be dealing with these disasters—when in fact, he is the one who is causing them! His purpose in initiating these regional or worldwide catastrophes is simple. He will loose the hordes of hell to cause unimaginable suffering, but without the masses of people who are affected knowing it was him who started it all. Then, after a turbulent period of sorrow, he will claim that he has the answer to the problem. All people need to do to receive his provision is to swear their perpetual allegiance to him.

It is not hard to imagine how this could happen. We have already seen a trial run of sorts with a recent pandemic. Consider this scenario, all of which could take place under the antichrist's authority, but without anyone except those directly involved knowing anything about his involvement. A laboratory develops a new virus, unprecedented in strength and scope. They also develop an antidote for the new pathogen. They release the virus and promote protocols that are supposed to mitigate its effects on people, when in fact, their directions do exactly the opposite. Those who follow what the experts tell them endure even greater suffering and death.

In the midst of the panic that ensues, the antichrist announces that due to the dauntless efforts of the scientists and researchers he has assembled, a vaccine has become available in record time—and it is free! The only stipulation is that people who receive the vaccine must be identified for accurate record-keeping purposes. Due to the dangerous nature of the health emergency, he has to know who is and who is not inoculated. The proof is a subcutaneous marker in the form of a microchip, inserted under the skin of the hand or the forehead. It contains all your biometric information, as well as your identity—all your important records are included. Thanks to AI, the chip, many times smaller than a grain of rice, also contains the ability to track your movements on a minute-by-minute basis. Everything is voluntary at this point. No coercion will be required, since fear of the virus will be all the motivation that multiplied millions need to get both the jab and the chip.

The same principle can be repeated regardless of the disaster that happens. Famine? Get the chip and receive food for you and your family. War? Qualify for evacuation from the danger zone if you are chipped. In every case, the antichrist will be the answer for the world's problems. His lust for power and control will be satisfied for a while. The relative period of calm will come to a conclusion with cataclysms that the world has never before witnessed. First Thessalonians 5:3 (KJV) says:

> For when they shall say, Peace and safety; then sudden destruction cometh upon them, as travail upon a woman with child; and they shall not escape.

When enough people have been deceived into thinking that the antichrist is their savior, things will become clear enough to those with eyes to see. It will be too late for them to change anything, even though they will come to regret the decisions they have made that led them to that point. The declension will happen with stunning swiftness, like a mighty bridge that has been eroded by wind and weather for many years before suddenly collapsing in an unrecoverable wreckage of concrete and steel. It is only after the antichrist has solidified his base of power that world conditions will take a decidedly nasty turn, the mask will come off, and the antichrist will reveal himself as the imposter and deceiver that he has always been.

Potential outcomes such as I have described make it easier to understand how the following verses could easily become reality—as Revelation 13:16-17 (KJV) states:

And he causeth all, both small and great, rich and poor, free and bond, to receive a mark in their right hand, or in their foreheads: and that no man might buy or sell, save he that had the mark, or the name of the beast, or the number of his name.

Previous generations could only speculate about how such a thing could ever happen, since the necessary technology to make it happen was not available. Now it is. Thanks to AI, whatever gaps may remain in the current technology can be quickly eliminated. What used to take years of development can now happen in months—or even in weeks.

During the recent pandemic, some health care experts wanted to use current technology to microchip people to keep track of their medical records. People objected to this proposal, and it was not implemented—but neither was it abandoned. The processes and procedures are already in development for when they will be needed by those in authority and accepted by the masses.

Let's say that a microchip is innocuous—only to be used in the same way they are already used to identify pets or personal property. It does not involve worship in any way. Would God exclude you from heaven for getting one? Of course not, but I don't think that is the right question. What if the same chip that tells you where your elderly family member who suffers from dementia is right now could be automatically altered to awaken latent capabilities that are not currently activated? What if the same technology that is promoted to help you can also become something that constrains you to do what you don't want to do?

The debate about which kind of microchip is available or will be available is not the real issue. All of it is nothing more than a precursor to the antichrist establishing his system of control and coercion. Resistance to all of this is coming from Christians—people who know their Bible. Remember that the force that is currently restraining the antichrist from establishing his rule is the Holy Spirit-filled Church.

Those who are familiar with biblical eschatology will have an aversion to any kind of chip or mark and, until they are taken out of the way, no world ruler will be able to implement his plan. When the Church is gone, the restraining factor will be removed, and this beastly system will be ushered into reality. Predictive Programing will make it easy for men and women to comply with it because they will have already been preconditioned to accept its inevitability. Many will accept the antichrist system in the future because they allow his spirit to operate today.

CHAPTER FIFTEEN

WARNING:
Watch for THIS

Good people get confused about Matthew 24 and 25, where Jesus gave very specific information regarding the end of the age. Matthew 24 is often called the mini apocalypse because in the first few verses, Jesus lays out the precise events of the last days, as they were later disclosed to John in Revelation 6. He began this discourse with a shocking prediction of the overthrow and destruction of the Temple. Matthew 24:3 (KJV) says:

> And as he sat upon the mount of Olives, the disciples came unto him privately, saying, Tell us, when shall these things be? and what shall be the sign of thy coming, and of the end of the world?

There were three questions:

- When will this happen?
- What will be the sign of Your coming?
- What is the sign of the end of the world?

Jesus did not always answer questions in the order in which they were asked. He would often answer in a way His listeners did not expect. Among the many dramatic evidences Jesus gave of the conditions surrounding His return (His triumphant return to the earth, not the blessed hope of the Church), was this, from Matthew 24:37-42 (KJV):

> *But as the days of Noah were, so shall also the coming of the Son of man be. For as in the days that were before the flood they were eating and drinking, marrying and giving in marriage, until the day that Noe entered into the ark, and knew not until the flood came, and took them all away; so shall also the coming of the Son of man be. Then shall two be in the field; the one shall be taken, and the other left. Two women shall be grinding at the mill; the one shall be taken, and the other left. Watch therefore: for ye know not what hour your Lord doth come.*

Jesus did not say it was wrong to eat, drink, get married, have a job, or fulfill other necessary responsibilities. What He was saying in this passage can be summarized by the last statement in it: "*Watch therefore: for ye know not what hour your Lord doth come.*"

He is talking about not being mindful of spiritual things in the midst of natural things. He's talking about not being aware of the potential of imminent judgment. People in Noah's day had no thought that judgment was coming. They were going through their days, working their jobs, and feeding their families—the same kinds of things that people do today—without a thought that anything would change. Some even mock the idea of the end of the age or the imminent return of our Savior. The Bible addresses this in 2 Peter 3:3-10 (KJV):

Knowing this first, that there shall come in the last days scoffers, walking after their own lusts, and saying, Where is the promise of his coming? for since the fathers fell asleep, all things continue as they were from the beginning of the creation. For this they willingly are ignorant of, that by the word of God the heavens were of old, and the earth standing out of the water and in the water: whereby the world that then was, being overflowed with water, perished: but the heavens and the earth, which are now, by the same word are kept in store, reserved unto fire against the day of judgment and perdition of ungodly men.

But, beloved, be not ignorant of this one thing, that one day is with the Lord as a thousand years, and a thousand years as one day. The Lord is not slack concerning his promise, as some men count slackness; but is longsuffering to us-ward, not willing that any should perish, but that all should come to repentance. But the day of the Lord will come as a thief in the night; in the which the heavens shall pass away with a great noise, and the elements shall melt with fervent heat, the earth also and the works that are therein shall be burned up.

Peter is saying the same thing that Jesus was communicating in Matthew 24 and 25. He forecasts that there will be scoffers, who taunt the faithful by asking why they can be so sure Jesus is coming, since He hasn't appeared yet. Peter was accurate in that prediction. Here is a solemn truth: God makes no promises that He does not fulfill.

- God said Jesus would come as a baby in Bethlehem, and He came.

- God said Jesus would be crucified and rise from the dead, and He was, and He did.

- God said Jesus would come again, and He will.

- God does not settle for being right two out of three times. He is faithful to His promises.

Peter also refers to the days of Noah, referring to the flood. The scoffers and mockers of Noah's day said the same things then that they do today. They ridicule the concept of the return of the King of kings and Lord of lords. They maintain that they must attend to much more important affairs than the obscure predictions of an uncertain and unknowable future event.

Peter reminds us that the world that was then was destroyed by water. He then says the world that is now will not be drowned, but it will be burned. He is right. The mockers are wrong. They insist Jesus is not coming, and they live like they believe their pronouncement is true. Peter says they are willfully ignorant. The reason for what seems like the delay in Jesus' return is not that God is unaware of the time, but because He is. He is patient, and He is awaiting the repentance of multitudes before the end-time countdown begins.

Let me reference one more witness—once again, the apostle Paul. Fifty percent of 2 Thessalonians references the end times directly, and even more of that letter makes indirect reference to the second coming of Jesus. Think about the urgency behind his words in 2 Thessalonians 3:14-15 (KJV), where he warned against those who lived as though Jesus was not coming:

> *And if any man obey not our word by this epistle, note that man, and have no company with him, that he*

may be ashamed. Yet count him not as an enemy, but admonish him as a brother.

Paul is not talking about someone in the world who questions Jesus' return. He is speaking of someone in the Church who does so. He goes on to say that other believers should not fellowship with those who live contrary to the expectation of His return. He does not say that because brothers and sisters may disagree on this issue that it disqualifies them from the kingdom of God. The reason is that complacency and carelessness are contagious. If you spend all your time with those who mind only worldly things, chances are good that you will begin to mind only worldly things, giving no thought to Jesus' coming. A serious study of the end times, whether from the teaching of Jesus, Peter, or Paul, can be summed up in one word: watch.

All scriptural eschatology (the part of theology that deals with the end times) emphasizes the concept of watchfulness. Every person who teaches Bible prophecy should center their instruction around this concept. Any eschatological teaching that does not emphasize the urgency of watching should be viewed as untrustworthy. This one word can keep you straight about the last days. As the old saying goes, we should live every day like it is our last—because one day we will be right.

WHY WATCH?

Let's take a look at what it means to watch and why. The word *imminent* means ready to take place or happening soon. It means to hang over one's head. It speaks of something ready to befall or overtake us. Ultimately it means that something is close at hand in its incidence.

It does not mean "soon," but it does mean that it could happen at any moment.

Here is an illustration of imminence and the urgency that it conveys. Imagine that you are a rebellious teenager. (For some of us, this exercise will be a little easier than for others.) Imagine that your parents are going out of town, and you decide to throw a party at your house (which is actually their house). The music is blaring, and a variety of activities are going on that you are certain your parents would never have allowed. The house is a mess. The driveway is full of vehicles. The backyard looks like a homeless encampment. In the midst of all this confusion, the phone rings. It's your dad. He tells you that their plans have changed unexpectedly and—they'll be home at *any moment*.

Your rebellious streak suddenly evaporates like a drop of water in the desert. Your expectation of a good time partying with your friends pops like an overinflated balloon, and it is replaced with an entirely different expectation. You begin a frantic flurry of activity that has nothing to do with fun and games. This is serious business. Your life and your future are at stake. You turn off the music, announce that the party is over, try to recruit some disappointed friends to help you clean up the disaster zone that your home has become, and kick everyone else out the same door you welcomed them in just a short time ago. What happened? You have had a revelation of imminence!

Now imagine that same scenario, but the message from your parents is quite different. The music is blaring, and the party is rocking as your parents tell you, "It looks like we are going to be gone longer than we planned." What's your reaction? You'd probably say, "Thanks, Mom and Dad! Call me when you're on your way!" Then you would end the call and tell everyone that it looks like the party just got a little more epic.

Imminence is a sound foundational doctrine concerning the return of Jesus, since an *at any moment* understanding can radically change our behavior. First John 3:3 (KJV) says, "*And every man that hath this hope in him purifieth himself, even as he is pure.*" Jesus spoke to this in Matthew 24:44-51 (KJV):

> *Therefore be ye also ready: for in such an hour as ye think not the Son of man cometh. Who then is a faithful and wise servant, whom his lord hath made ruler over his household, to give them meat in due season? Blessed is that servant, whom his lord when he cometh shall find so doing. Verily I say unto you, That he shall make him ruler over all his goods. But and if that evil servant shall say in his heart, My lord delayeth his coming; and shall begin to smite his fellowservants, and to eat and drink with the drunken; the lord of that servant shall come in a day when he looketh not for him, and in an hour that he is not aware of, and shall cut him asunder, and appoint him his portion with the hypocrites: there shall be weeping and gnashing of teeth.*

When approaching a subject that even the apostle Paul, in 1 Corinthians 15:51, called a *mystery,* there should be a level of humility that accompanies our study. There are some things that we may not understand or that seem to be contradictory, but there are others which are indisputably clear. We must anchor ourselves in the certainty of what the Bible teaches before we venture out to discover new revelation or endeavor to give our opinion.

What should we do when confronted with seeming contradictions? We cling to sound doctrine, and humbly ask God for clear understanding. If any new information seeks to take us away from our anchor of the word of God, we should disregard it no matter how fascinating it may be.

There is one theme about the appearing of the Lord Jesus Christ that should be our anchor when seeking to understand the events, the signs, and the prophetic forecasts of the last days: imminence. Throughout the New Testament, we read words such as *watch, look, wait,* and *quickly.* All these terms describe the principle of imminence.

22 SCRIPTURAL PROOFS THAT JESUS COULD APPEAR AT ANY MOMENT

1. *"Watch therefore, for ye know neither the day nor the hour wherein the Son of man cometh"* (Matthew 25:13 KJV).

2. *"But of that day and hour knoweth no man, no, not the angels of heaven, but my Father only"* (Matthew 24:36 KJV).

3. *"Watch therefore: for ye know not what hour your Lord doth come. But know this, that if the goodman of the house had known in what watch the thief would come, he would have watched, and would not have suffered his house to be broken up. Therefore be ye also ready: for in such an hour as ye think not the Son of man cometh. Who then is a faithful and wise servant, whom his lord hath made ruler over his household, to give them meat in due season? Blessed is that servant, whom his lord when he cometh shall find so doing"* (Matthew 24:42-46 KJV).

4. *"Take ye heed, watch and pray; for ye know not when the time is. For the Son of Man is as a man taking a far journey, who left his house, and gave authority to his servants, and to every man his work, and commanded the porter to watch. Watch ye therefore: for ye know not when the master of the house cometh, at even, or at midnight, or at the cockcrowing, or in the morning: Lest coming suddenly he find you sleeping. And what I say unto you I say unto all, Watch"* (Mark 13:33-37 KJV).

5. *"Knowing the time, that now it is high time to awake out of sleep: for now is our salvation nearer than when we believed. The night is far spent, the day is at hand: let us therefore, cast off the works of darkness, and let us put on the armour of light"* (Romans 13:11-12 KJV).

6. *"And the God of peace shall bruise Satan under your feet shortly"* (Romans 16:20 KJV).

7. *"So that ye come behind in no gift; waiting for the coming of our Lord Jesus Christ"* (1 Corinthians 1:7 KJV).

8. *"For our conversation is in heaven; from whence also we look for the Saviour, the Lord Jesus Christ"* (Philippians 3:20 KJV).

9. *"Let your moderation be known unto all men. The Lord is at hand"* (Philippians 4:5 KJV).

10. *"And to wait for his Son from heaven, whom he raised from the dead, even Jesus, which delivered us from the wrath to come"* (1 Thessalonians 1:10 KJV).

11. *"Therefore let us not sleep, as do others; but let us watch and be sober"* (1 Thessalonians 5:6 KJV).

12. *"That thou keep this commandment without spot, unrebukable, until the appearing of our Lord Jesus Christ"* (1 Timothy 6:14 KJV).

13. *"Looking for that blessed hope, and the glorious appearing of the great God and our Saviour Jesus Christ"* (Titus 2:13 KJV).

14. *"So Christ was once offered to bear the sins of many; and unto them that look for him shall he appear the second time without sin unto salvation"* (Hebrews 9:28 KJV).

15. *"Let us consider one another to provoke unto love and to good works: Not forsaking the assembling of ourselves together, as the manner of some is; but exhorting one another: and so much the more, as ye see the day approaching"* (Hebrews 10:24-25 KJV).

16. *"For yet a little while, and He that shall come will come, and will not tarry"* (Hebrews 10:37 KJV).

17. *"Be patient therefore, brethren, unto the coming of the Lord. Behold, the husbandman waiteth for the precious fruit of the earth, and hath long patience for it, until he receive the early and latter rain. Be ye also patient; stablish your hearts: for the coming of the Lord draweth nigh. Grudge not one against another, brethren, lest ye be condemned: behold, the judge standeth before the door"* (James 5:7-9 KJV).

18. *"Wherefore gird up the loins of your mind, be sober, and hope to the end for the grace that is to be brought unto you at the revelation of Jesus Christ"* (1 Peter 1:13 KJV).

19. *"But the end of all things is at hand: be ye therefore sober, and watch unto prayer"* (1 Peter 4:7 KJV).

20. *"Behold, I come quickly: hold that fast which thou hast, that no man take thy crown"* (Revelation 3:11 KJV).

21. *"Behold, I come quickly: blessed is he that keepeth the sayings of the prophecy of this book"* (Revelation 22:7 KJV).

22. *"He which testifieth these things saith, Surely I come quickly. Amen. Even so, come, Lord Jesus"* (Revelation 22:20 KJV).

There is one word that can summarize all New Testament eschatology: *WATCH!* This attitude was central in the teachings of Jesus and the apostles. This is our anchor. Anything that seeks to pull us away from an urgently watchful attitude should be refuted. If any teaching suggests that even one prophecy has to come to pass before Jesus can return for His Church, it does not conform to the doctrine of imminence.

You may have noticed that I haven't mentioned the three different doctrinal positions regarding the rapture of the Church (pre-, mid-, post-tribulation). When we take imminence seriously, such debate becomes unnecessary. All views but one require many prophecies to be fulfilled before Jesus can return for His Church. In doing so, they rob us of imminence.

There are those who say that they can maintain an imminent attitude because they know that they could die at any moment and meet

Jesus after death. This is like trying to fix a car engine with duct tape. It may work, but not for long. This attitude unwittingly robs us of the exquisite diamond of the blessed hope of the Church and replaces it with the cubic zirconia of physical death. It is true that, should the Lord tarry, we will all meet death. The problem with death being our expectation is that according to the scriptures I listed, Jesus didn't want us looking for death. He certainly didn't want us looking for the antichrist. *He wants us to look for Him!*

It only takes a few moments of fearless introspection to know why. Take some time to contemplate your death. Think of all the ways it could happen and what it would be like to die, to leave this world and to meet Jesus in heaven. Keep in mind that even though death has been conquered through Christ's resurrection, it is still an enemy, and the last one to be destroyed, according to 1 Corinthians 15:26. In contrast to that, take a few moments to consider this fact: *at any moment,* Jesus could split the eastern sky and catch you up to meet Him in the clouds. There's a difference—the same kind of difference you would experience by taking a trip accompanied by an enemy or by a friend!

The early Church was so expectant that Jesus could come at any moment that they greeted one another with the word *Maranatha,* which means, *Our Lord, Come.* It's a petition that every Christian had on the tip of their tongue. This is how they said *hello* and *goodbye.* If they thought they were so close to the appearing of Jesus, how much more should we be looking for it and expecting it?

A DIFFERENT MARK

What happens to any sports team when a two-minute warning is given? Does anyone slow down, bury their heads in the sand, or disengage from the game? Not if they are serious about competing! The last few seconds of any game are always the most exciting. No matter how tired everyone is, they kick into high gear because they know that they only have a few moments left to make a difference. Like a two-minute warning, the revelation of imminence causes Christians to push past their pain, fight even harder, and give it all they've got. We have been called to look for His imminent return and occupy until He comes.

Don't be duped by the antichrist spirit. It's the spirit of the world— the spirit of this age. The antichrist will take advantage of people who aren't watching for the return of Christ. Anyone not looking for Christ is susceptible to receiving the mark. Those who allow themselves to be drawn away from expecting the appearing of Jesus at any moment are candidates for deception of all kinds. We are to be fully alert, with our lights shining bright, and we should never allow ourselves to be seduced to sleep by any spirit that operates contrary to the Holy Spirit.

The first *mark* mentioned in the Bible is the *mark of Cain* (see Genesis 4:15). He was bringing a halfhearted offering. His mark had to do with envy over prosperity. I find it interesting that the last mark in the Bible will also deal with money. The mark that Cain received was a consequence of his murderous envy. This mark deals with bringing God less than you know in your heart that God requires. If you don't give God what belongs to Him, you become easily marked. What you need to know now is that satan is an imitator. He has a mark because he's trying to mimic the God of all creation who also has a mark. Did you know that God marks His people?

Ezekiel saw this scenario about imminent judgment:

> *He cried also in mine ears with a loud voice, saying,*
> *Cause them that have charge over the city to draw*
> *near, even every man with his destroying weapon in*

his hand. And, behold, six men came from the way of the higher gate, which lieth toward the north, and every man a slaughter weapon in his hand; and one man among them was clothed with linen, with a writer's inkhorn by his side: and they went in, and stood beside the brazen altar. And the glory of the God of Israel was gone up from the cherub, whereupon he was, to the threshold of the house.

And he called to the man clothed with linen, which had the writer's inkhorn by his side; and the Lord said unto him, Go through the midst of the city, through the midst of Jerusalem, and set a mark upon the foreheads of the men that sigh and that cry for all the abominations that be done in the midst thereof. And to the others he said in mine hearing, Go ye after him through the city, and smite: let not your eye spare, neither have ye pity: slay utterly old and young, both maids, and little children, and women: but come not near any man upon whom is the mark; and begin at my sanctuary. Then they began at the ancient men which were before the house (Ezekiel 9:1-6 KJV).

God knows those who are His. Let hell attack. You are sealed in the hand of the Almighty God of Heaven and Earth. You need not worry about the mark of the beast because you are already marked. The space has been taken. You have been reserved for the worship of the true Christ, not the antichrist. You have been bought and paid for. You belong to Jesus and He is about to return to claim what's His!

CHAPTER SIXTEEN

SATAN'S END-TIME STRATEGY EXPOSED

We find out more details about the strategy of the antichrist in Daniel 7:25 (KJV):

> *And he shall speak great words against the most High,*
> *and shall wear out the saints of the most High, and*
> *think to change times and laws.*

The antichrist's goal is to wear the saints down. Due to the lateness of the hour in which we live, I believe the antichrist has been born and is walking the earth right now. However, he is unable to reveal himself because of the restraining influence of the Church. His goal will be the same regardless of when he appears—he will attempt to wear out the saints. Never forget that the goal of the antichrist spirit is to weary you. Don't let him!

How does the spirit of antichrist accomplish that? What is it that causes the saints to grow weary? We don't grow frustrated because we question *what* God can do. We know our God can do exceedingly abundantly above all we ask or think according to His power at work within us. He is, after all, Jehovah, Yahweh, the Lion of the Tribe of

Judah. He is all-powerful! We are not wearied by questions concerning His ability.

However, there is another question—*when*? There is a question that can distract us from the intention and purpose that God has for us. There is a question that can weary the saints of God as they lay in a hospital bed, struggling with a diagnosis. There is a question that can weary a heart that is living in a home that is not all that God has called it to be. It is not about what God can do, but *when* God will do it. When will the miracle break through? When will the manifestation come? These are questions that can weary any believer. What is it about waiting that wearies us? Anyone who has ever had a vigil in a hospital waiting area knows that what I'm saying is true. There is absolutely nothing for you to do except wait, and yet it seems as though it is the most wearying thing you have ever done. Waiting can be wearying—especially when the end of the wait is unknown.

In Exodus 32, God's people are at Mount Sinai after having been delivered from Egyptian bondage. The mountain is ablaze. Smoke rises to the heavens. The ground is shaking, and a voice speaks like thunder. Instead of maintaining his distance as everyone else was doing, Moses goes up the mountain into all that chaos. He is gone for over a month. Nobody has seen him; nobody has a clue what has happened to him. The consensus is that he must be dead. Exodus 32:1 (KJV) says:

> *And when the people saw that Moses delayed to come down out of the mount, the people gathered themselves together unto Aaron, and said unto him, Up, make us gods, which shall go before us; for as for this Moses, the man that brought us up out of the land of Egypt, we wot not what is become of him.*

They became impatient because they had to wait longer than they thought they should. Someone got the bright idea that they should go back to what they just left: bondage in Egypt. The incident with the golden calf followed.

Israel's first king became impatient. First Samuel 13:8-13 (KJV) tells this story:

> *And he tarried seven days, according to the set time that Samuel had appointed: but Samuel came not to Gilgal; and the people were scattered from him. And Saul said, Bring hither a burnt offering to me, and peace offerings. And he offered the burnt offering. And it came to pass, that as soon as he had made an end of offering the burnt offering, behold, Samuel came; and Saul went out to meet him, that he might salute him. And Samuel said, What hast thou done?*
>
> *And Saul said, Because I saw that the people were scattered from me, and that thou camest not with the days appointed, and that the Philistines gathered themselves together at Michmash; therefore said I, The Philistines will come down now upon me to Gilgal, and I have not made supplication unto the Lord: I forced myself therefore, and offered a burnt offering. And Samuel said to Saul, Thou hast done foolishly: thou hast not kept the commandment of the Lord thy God, which he commanded thee: for now would the Lord have established thy kingdom upon Israel for ever.*

Samuel called what Saul did foolish. It wasn't that Saul did not wait; it was that Saul was not *prepared* to wait. He was prepared to wait for as long as he thought he should wait for Samuel to show up. However, when the prophet did not come as expected, Saul was uncertain about what to do. He did not realize that the thing he needed to do was to do *nothing* until Samuel appeared.

Once again, I remind you of what Peter said about impatience and its consequences:

> *Knowing this first, that there shall come in the last days scoffers, walking after their own lusts, and saying, Where is the promise of his coming? For since the fathers fell asleep, all things continue as they were from the beginning of the creation* (2 Peter 3:3-4 KJV).

Scoffers are sent to weary you in waiting. Every generation has had its scoffers who mock the saints for believing that Jesus is coming. Listen to this message from Jesus Himself in Luke 12:35-45 (KJV):

> *Let your loins be girded about, and your lights burning; and ye yourselves like unto men that wait for their lord, when he will return from the wedding; that when he cometh and knocketh, they may open unto him immediately. Blessed are those servants, whom the lord when he cometh shall find watching: verily I say unto you, that he shall gird himself, and make them to sit down to meat, and will come forth and serve them. And if he shall come in the second watch, or come in the third watch, and find them so, blessed are those servants.*
>
> *And this know, that if the goodman of the house had known what hour the thief would come, he would have watched, and not have suffered his house to be broken through. Be ye therefore ready also: for the Son of man*

cometh at an hour when ye think not. Then Peter said unto him, Lord, speakest thou this parable unto us, or even to all? And the Lord said, Who then is that faithful and wise steward, whom his lord shall make ruler over his household, to give them their portion of meat in due season?

Blessed is that servant, whom his lord when he cometh shall find so doing. Of a truth I say unto you, that he will make him ruler over all that he hath. But and if that servant say in his heart, **My lord delayeth his coming;** *and shall begin to beat the menservants and maidens, and to eat and drink, and to be drunken; The lord of that servant will come in a day when he looketh not for him, and at an hour when he is not aware, and will cut him in sunder, and will appoint him his portion with the unbelievers.*

According to Hebrews 6:12, it is through faith *and* patience that we inherit the promises. Satan knows that a prime time to tempt you is during a period of waiting. Between the time you believe that you receive and the time that you actually possess the promise, the devil will whisper lies in your mind. He attempts to weary you in the waiting.

One of the greatest temptations of disciples of any age is that they think the promises of God will always produce instantaneous results. When things don't happen according to their timetable, they become discouraged and are tempted to quit. Listen to this admonition from Luke 19:13 (KJV):

And he called his ten servants, and delivered them ten pounds, and said unto them, Occupy till I come.

Whether the appearing of Jesus is near or distant, we have business—kingdom business—to accomplish. Keep fulfilling your God-given purpose whether it lasts for days or decades. The parable of the ten virgins drives this home:

> *Then shall the kingdom of heaven be likened unto ten virgins, which took their lamps, and went forth to meet the bridegroom. And five of them were wise, and five were foolish. They that were foolish took their lamps, and took no oil with them: but the wise took oil in their vessels with their lamps. While the bridegroom tarried, they all slumbered and slept. And at midnight there was a cry made, Behold, the bridegroom cometh; go ye out to meet him. Then all those virgins arose, and trimmed their lamps.*
>
> *And the foolish said unto the wise, Give us of your oil; for our lamps are gone out. But the wise answered, saying, Not so; lest there be not enough for us and you: but go ye rather to them that sell, and buy for yourselves. And while they went to buy, the bridegroom came; and **they that were ready** went in with him to the marriage: and the door was shut. Afterward came also the other virgins, saying, Lord, Lord, open to us. But he answered and said, Verily I say unto you, I know not (Matthew 25:1-12).*

In verse 2, the Greek word for foolish is *moros*, from which we get our English word *moron*. There are many interpretations concerning who the 10 virgins are, but there is one central truth. Jesus is saying to all of us, *watch* and be prepared to watch for however long it takes. Regardless of who the virgins represent, there is one reality of which we can all be sure: *Those who hold their faith through the darkness will eventually be vindicated.* It can be easy for anyone to become weary, regardless of the thoroughness of their preparation. These virgins all had one thing in common—they all slept. They all are virgins, they all have lamps that work, and they are all looking for the bridegroom. These ten are the elite, the best of the best. They were all expecting the same outcome, but five were wise and five were foolish.

BE PREPARED TO *WAIT*

The point that this parable makes is that the Christian life requires a faith that is prepared to wait. What does it mean to be ready? If we are going to be ready for the triumph of faith, we must have a faith that can hold out beyond midnight. We must have a faith that is alert enough and strong enough to *outlast* weariness. The five foolish virgins had no staying power. They miscalculated the strain of the enterprise on which they set out. The five wise virgins had considered all the possibilities. They knew that the bridegroom might be delayed on the road and might not arrive as soon as they had hoped.

There are plenty of people who have an experience with God's grace, and they blaze for a moment in His glory, but the next time you see them, their lamp has gone out. Things did not happen as they expected. Things took longer than they thought they would or should. They thought prayer would bring immediate change. They may burn brightly, but they burn out when the enemies in their lives don't bow as quickly as they'd like.

We must live as though Christ could return at any moment, and plan as though He won't return for a hundred years. Prepare and plan. The faith that Jesus asks of us is the faith that can hold on through all the delays of His purpose. If you find yourself at the midnight hour, you need to have a faith that will trust God regardless of the circumstances. The deadline may come and go, but our faith needs to remain the same. God does not change, and our trust in Him should not change, either. Faith, after all, is trust. Can we hold on? Can we go on past the time we thought we would be free and rest knowing God will see us through?

All the virgins in this parable slept. The five wise virgins were calm and confident. They were so confident and free of care that they could fall asleep, even though the object of their expectation had not yet arrived. Their calm was real rest and not lazy slumber. Peter slept on the eve of the execution Herod planned for him. He trusted that God would deliver him, and his faith was vindicated.

The antichrist spirit proceeds from the prince of darkness. His strategy is to keep you from having a sufficient store of oil. Ephesians 5:14-20 (KJV) tells us how to stay prepared:

> *Wherefore he saith, Awake thou that sleepest, and arise from the dead, and Christ shall give thee light. See then that ye walk circumspectly, not as fools, but as wise, Redeeming the time, because the days are evil. Wherefore be ye not unwise, but understanding what the will of the Lord is. And be not drunk with wine, wherein is excess; but be filled with the Spirit; Speaking to yourselves in psalms and hymns and spiritual songs, singing and making melody in your heart to the Lord; Giving thanks always for all things unto God and the Father in the name of our Lord Jesus Christ.*

I have done my share of traveling. One truth that has saved me a lot of trouble is to fill up my vehicle's fuel tank while I still have half a tank of fuel remaining. I can't tell you how many times I've passed a gas station thinking I'd have plenty of time to fuel up later, only to find myself in an anxious situation because I didn't make sure my tank was full when I had the opportunity. Isaiah 40:31 (KJV) says:

> But they that wait upon the Lord shall renew their strength; they shall mount up with wings as eagles; they shall run, and not be weary; and they shall walk, and not faint.

Don't wait until it is too late to fill up spiritually. It may be inconvenient, and it may take a little extra effort, but we must do it while we have the time. Let's be patient and stay prepared!

Whether it's artificial intelligence, aliens, or the antichrist, we will not cower in our cultural corner and hope for the best. We will not abandon this generation because we know it's all going to eventually come down anyway. The ethical and moral dilemmas we'll face won't be easy, but neither were the challenges confronted by the early Church or by countless faithful followers of Christ throughout history. We must rise up to face these challenges head-on knowing that:

> Ye are of God, little children, and have overcome them: because greater is he that is in you, than he that is in the world (1 John 4:4 KJV).

APPENDIX A

PRESIDENT'S STATEMENT ANNOUNCING THE USE OF THE A-BOMB AT HIROSHIMA ON AUGUST 6, 1945

Sixteen hours ago an American airplane dropped one bomb on Hiroshima, an important Japanese Army base. That bomb had more power than 20,000 tons of T.N.T. It had more than two thousand times the blast power of the British "Grand Slam" which is the largest bomb ever yet used in the history of warfare.

The Japanese began the war from the air at Pearl Harbor. They have been repaid many fold. And the end is not yet. With this bomb we have now added a new and revolutionary increase in destruction to supplement the growing power of our armed forces. In their present form these bombs are now in production and even more powerful forms are in development.

It is an atomic bomb. It is a harnessing of the basic power of the universe. The force from which the sun draws its power has been loosed against those who brought war to the Far East.

Before 1939, it was the accepted belief of scientists that it was theoretically possible to release atomic energy. But no one knew any practical method of doing it. By 1942, however, we knew that the Germans were working feverishly to find a way to add atomic energy to the other engines of war with which they hoped to enslave the world. But they failed. We may be grateful to Providence that the Germans got the V-1's and V-2's late and in limited quantities and even more grateful that they did not get the atomic bomb at all.

The battle of the laboratories held fateful risks for us as well as the battles of the air, land and sea, and we have now won the battle of the laboratories as we have won the other battles.

Beginning in 1940, before Pearl Harbor, scientific knowledge useful in war was pooled between the United States and Great Britain, and many priceless helps to our victories have come from that arrangement. Under that general policy the research on the atomic bomb was begun. With American and British scientists working together we entered the race of discovery against the Germans.

The United States had available the large number of scientists of distinction in the many needed areas of knowledge. It had the tremendous industrial and financial resources necessary for the project and they could be devoted to it without undue impairment of other vital war work. In the United States the laboratory work and the production plants, on which a substantial start had already been made, would be out of reach of enemy bombing, while at that time Britain was exposed to constant air attack and was still threatened with the possibility of invasion. For these reasons Prime Minister Churchill and President Roosevelt agreed that it was wise to carry on the project here. We now have two great plants and many lesser works devoted to the production of atomic power. Employment during peak construction numbered 125,000 and over 65,000 individuals are even now engaged in operating the plants. Many have worked there for two and a half years. Few know what they have been producing. They see great quantities of material going in and they see nothing coming out of these plants, for the physical size of the explosive charge is exceedingly small. We have spent two billion dollars on the greatest scientific gamble in history-and won.

But the greatest marvel is not the size of the enterprise, its secrecy, nor its cost, but the achievement of scientific brains in putting together infinitely complex pieces of knowledge held by many men in different fields of science into a workable plan. And hardly less marvelous has been the capacity of industry to design, and of labor to operate, the machines and methods to do things never done before so that the brain child of many minds came forth in physical shape and performed as it was supposed to do. Both science and industry worked under the direction of the United States Army, which achieved a unique success in managing so diverse a problem in the advancement of knowledge in an amazingly short time. It is doubtful if such another combination could be got together in the world. What has been done is the greatest achievement of organized science in history. It was done under high pressure and without failure.

We are now prepared to obliterate more rapidly and completely every productive enterprise the Japanese have above ground in any city. We shall destroy their docks, their factories, and their communications. Let there be no mistake; we shall completely destroy Japan's power to make war.

It was to spare the Japanese people from utter destruction that the ultimatum of July 26 was issued at Potsdam. Their leaders promptly rejected that ultimatum. If they do not now accept our terms they may expect a rain of ruin from the air, the like of which has never been seen on this earth. Behind this air attack will follow sea and land forces in such numbers and power as they have not yet seen and with the fighting skill of which they are already well aware.

The Secretary of War, who has kept in personal touch with all phases of the project, will immediately make public a statement giving further details.

His statement will give facts concerning the sites at Oak Ridge near Knoxville, Tennessee, and at Richland near Pasco, Washington, and an installation near Santa Fe, New Mexico. Although the workers at the sites have been making materials to be used in producing the greatest destructive force in history they have not themselves been in danger beyond that of many other occupations, for the utmost care has been taken of their safety.

The fact that we can release atomic energy ushers in a new era in man's understanding of nature's forces. Atomic energy may in the future supplement the power that now comes from coal, oil, and falling water, but at present it cannot be produced on a basis to compete with them commercially. Before that comes there must be a long period of intensive research.

It has never been the habit of the scientists of this country or the policy of this Government to withhold from the world scientific knowledge. Normally, therefore, everything about the work with atomic energy would be made public.

But under present circumstances it is not intended to divulge the technical processes of production or all the military applications, pending further examination of possible methods of protecting us and the rest of the world from the danger of sudden destruction.

I shall recommend that the Congress of the United States consider promptly the establishment of an appropriate commission to control the production and use of atomic power within the United States. I shall give further consideration and make further recommendations to the Congress as to how atomic power can become a powerful and forceful influence towards the maintenance of world peace.[36]

NOTE: This statement was released in Washington. It was drafted before the President left Germany, and Secretary of War Stimson was authorized to release it when the bomb was delivered. On August 6, while returning from the Potsdam Conference aboard the U.S.S.

Augusta, the President was handed a message from Secretary Stimson informing him that the bomb had been dropped at 7:15 p.m. on August 5.

APPENDIX B

U.S. AIR FORCE FACT SHEET CONCERNING UFOS AND PROJECT BLUE BOOK

The following is a copy of the US Air Force Fact Sheet distributed by Wright-Patterson AFB in Ohio, January 1985 concerning the termination of Project Blue Book.

> On December 17, 1969, the Secretary of the Air Force announced the termination of Project BLUE BOOK, the Air Force program for the investigation of UFOS.
>
> From 1947 to 1969, a total of 12, 618 sightings were reported to Project BLUE BOOK. Of these 701 remain "Unidentified." The project was headquartered at Wright-Patterson Air Force Base, whose personnel no longer receive, document, or investigate UFO reports.
>
> The decision to discontinue UFO investigations was based on an evaluation of a report prepared by the University of Colorado entitled, "Scientific Study of Unidentified Flying Objects;" a review of the University of Colorado's report by the National Academy of Sciences; past UFO

studies and Air Force experience investigating UFO reports during the '40s, '50s, and '60s.

As a result of these investigations and studies and experience gained from investigating UFO reports since 1948, the conclusions of Project BLUE BOOK are:(1) no UFO reported, investigated, and evaluated by the Air Force has ever given any indication of threat to our national security;(2) there has been no evidence submitted to or discovered by the Air Force that sightings categorized as "unidentified" represent technological developments or principles beyond the range of present-day scientific knowledge; and(3) there has been no evidence indicating that sightings categorized as "unidentified" are extraterrestrial vehicles.

With the termination of Project BLUE BOOK, the Air Force regulations establishing and controlling the program for investigating and analyzing UFOs were rescinded. Documentation regarding the former BLUE BOOK investigation has been permanently transferred to the Military Reference Branch, National Archives and Records Administration, Washington, DC 20408, and is available for public review and analysis.

Since Project BLUE BOOK was closed, nothing has happened to indicate that the Air Force ought to resume investigating UFOs. Because of the considerable cost to the Air Force in the past, and the tight funding of Air Force needs today, there is no likelihood the Air Force will become involved with UFO investigation again.

There are a number of universities and professional scientific organizations, such as the American Association for the Advancement of Science, which have considered UFO phenomena during periodic meetings and seminars. In addition, a list of private organizations interested in aerial phenomena may be found in Gayle's Encyclopedia of Associations (edition 8, vol-. 1, pp. 432-433). Such timely review of the situation by private groups ensures that sound evidence will not be overlooked by the scientific community.

A person calling the base to report a UFO is advised to contact a private or professional organization (as mentioned above) or to contact a local law enforcement agency if the caller feels his or her public safety is endangered.

Periodically, it is erroneously stated that the remains of extraterrestrial visitors are or have been stored at Wright-Patterson AFB. There are not now nor ever have been, any extraterrestrial visitors or equipment on Wright-Patterson Air Force Base.[37]

UFO CONGRESSIONAL TESTIMONY[38]

In July of 2023, the United States House Committee on Oversight and Accountability held a hearing on the national security and public safety implications of UAPs (Unknown Arial Phenomena). Many witnesses have come out with information on what they have experienced as a result of expanded whistleblower protections.

Are these witnesses credible?

Is the government covering up information about UAPs and alien lifeforms?

Below you will be able to read the actual congressional record and decide for yourself.

SUBCOMMITTEE HEARING ON UNIDENTIFIED ANOMALOUS PHENOMENA: IMPLICATIONS ON NATIONAL SECURITY, PUBLIC SAFETY, AND GOVERNMENT TRANSPARENCY

Witnesses and testimonies:

Ryan Graves

Executive Director of Americans for Safe Aerospace

Chairman Grothman, Ranking Member Garcia, distinguished Members of the House Oversight Subcommittee on National Security, the Border, and Foreign Affairs, Representatives Burchett and Luna, thank you for holding the first public hearing on UAP to hear from military pilots and whistleblowers.

My name is Ryan "FOBS" Graves and I am a former F-18 pilot with over a decade of service in the U.S. Navy, including two deployments in Operation Enduring Freedom and Operation Inherent Resolve. I have witnessed advanced UAP on multiple sensor systems firsthand, and I'm here to voice the concerns of countless commercial aircrew and military veterans who have confided their similar encounters with me.

I can tell you that advanced UAP are a national security and an aviation safety problem.

It has been more than a decade since my squadron began witnessing advanced UAP demonstrating complex maneuvers on a regular basis, and we still don't have answers. I founded Americans for Safe Aerospace to create a center of support, research, and public education for aircrew impacted by UAP encounters. We now have nearly 5,000 members and are actively working with more than 30 UAP witnesses who have approached us. I am also the Chair of the UAP Integration and Outreach Committee for the American Institute of Aeronautics and Astronautics, where we have assembled a volunteer team of almost 80 PhDs and aerospace engineers dedicated to tackling the science around this issue.

Today, I would like to center our discussion around three critical issues that demand our immediate attention and concerted action:

1. As we convene here, UAP are in our airspace, but they are grossly underreported. These sightings are not rare or isolated; they are routine. Military aircrews and commercial pilots, trained observers whose lives depend on accurate identification, are frequently witnessing these phenomena.

2. The stigma attached to UAP is real and powerful and challenges national security. It silences commercial pilots who fear professional repercussions, discourages witnesses, and is only compounded by recent government claims questioning the credibility of eyewitness testimony.

3. The government knows more about UAP than shared publicly, and excessive classification practices keep crucial information hidden. There's a lack of transparency around UAP that's unsettling. Since 2021, all UAP videos are classified as secret or above. This level of secrecy not only impedes our understanding but fuels speculation and mistrust.

My experience: UAP encounters in W-72

I joined the U.S. Navy in 2009. As a pilot, I was trained to be an expert observer, tasked with identifying any aircraft within our operating area. In 2014, I was near Virginia Beach as part of VFA-11, a Navy Fighter/Attack Squadron made up of F/A-18F Super Hornets. Upon an upgrade to our radar system, we began to detect unknown objects in our airspace. Initially dismissed as software glitches, we soon corroborated these radar tracks with infrared sensors, confirming their physical presence.

Over time, UAP sightings became an open secret among our aircrew. They were a common occurrence, seen by most of my colleagues on radar and occasionally up close. The sightings were so frequent that they became part of daily briefs.

A pivotal incident occurred during an air combat training mission in Warning Area W-72, an exclusive block of airspace ten miles east of Virginia Beach. All traffic into the training area goes through a single GPS point at a set altitude. Just at the moment the two jets crossed the threshold, one of the pilots saw a dark gray cube inside of a clear sphere—motionless against the wind, fixed directly at the entry point. The jets, only 100 feet apart, were forced to take evasive action. They terminated the mission immediately and returned to base. Our squadron submitted a safety report, but there was no official acknowledgement of the incident and no further mechanism to report the sightings.

Advanced UAP defy conventional explanation

The UAP we encountered and tracked on multiple sensors behaved in ways that surpassed our understanding and technology. The UAP could accelerate at speeds up to Mach 1, hold their position against hurricane-force winds, and outlast our fighter jets, operating continuously throughout the day. They did not have any visible means of lift, control surfaces, or propulsion—nothing that resembled normal aircraft with wings, flaps, or engines. I am a formally trained engineer and I have no explanation for this.

Recently, I have received confirmation that these encounters were also a shock to the chain of command from one of our advisors at ASA, Rear Admiral Tim Gallaudet, former head of National Oceanic and Atmospheric Administration, and Oceanographer of the Navy.

While serving as an Admiral with Fleet Forces Command, he received a classified email on SIPRNET in 2015 from his boss, the Operations Commander, to all 1- and 2-star Admiral subordinates. The title of the email was "Urgent safety of flight issue." He attached the now famous GO-FAST UAP video from a Navy F/A-18, asking if anyone knew their origin, and expressed safety of flight concerns about multiple near mid-air collisions with UAP in the early warning area off Virginia Beach where my encounters occurred, noting they might shut down the exercise for safety reasons.

Admiral Gallaudet reviewed it with his deputy. The next day, the email was removed from his system and that of his deputy, and despite meeting with this group routinely in person, no one ever discussed it. He presumes the email was removed in connection with a classified special access program. He couldn't believe there was no discussion of an urgent safety of flight issue. He has stated publicly that after seeing the report, he didn't believe these UAP represent any known human technology.

Aircrews along the East Coast continue to encounter advanced UAP nearly a decade later, and the identity of these UAP remains unknown.

Americans for Safe Aerospace aircrew and military UAP witness program

Recognizing the need for action and answers, I founded Americans for Safe Aerospace, which now has nearly 5,000 members. What I did not anticipate was how many UAP military veteran and commercial aircrew witnesses would reach out to us. The organization has since become a haven for more than 30 UAP witnesses who were previously unspoken due to the absence of a safe intake process. Most do not want to speak publicly. They are afraid of professional consequences. They just want to add their account to the data set.

Commercial pilots

The majority of witnesses are commercial pilots at major airlines. Often they are veterans with decades of flying experience. Pilots are reporting UAP at altitudes that appear to be above them at 40,000 feet, potentially in low earth orbit or in the grey zone below the Karman line, making inexplicable maneuvers, like right hand turns and retrograde orbits, or j-hooks. Sometimes these reports are recurring, with numerous recent sightings north of Hawaii and the North Atlantic.

What commercial pilots tell us can defy belief, often beginning with an apology like, "I apologize, I realize this will sound crazy." I have met with highly credible commercial pilots at major airlines with decades of experience, often veterans, who describe UAP operating at altitudes that appear to be above them at 40,000 feet, potentially in low earth orbit or in the grey zone below the Karman line, making inexplicable maneuvers, like right hand turns and retrograde orbits, or j-hooks. Sometimes these reports are recurring, with numerous recent sightings north of Hawaii and the North Atlantic. They are trained observers, often former military pilots, who say they understand Starlink flares and are adamant that is not the explanation.

Other domain military witnesses

Other veterans are also coming forward to us regarding UAP encounters in our airspace and oceans. Veterans from all branches of service, who are authorized to come forward by the NDAA of 2023 to Congress and the All-domain Anomaly Resolution Office, are hesitant to do so due to stigma and a confusing process within government. Currently, there is no public-facing way for them to report their accounts. We are filling that gap.

The most compelling involve observations of UAP by multiple witnesses and sensor systems, with supporting documentation or a roadmap to find it. I believe these accounts are only scratching the surface and more will share their experiences once it is safe to do so. In multiple cases, contemporaneous notifications were made up the chain of command, and in several, sensor data was escalated for analysis and there were profound irregularities in how the data was handled.

Conclusion

There are credible reports from both military and commercial aircrew of unidentified objects in our military and commercial airspace occurring with regularity.

The UAP Task Force reported in 2021 that there were 11 near misses with UAP and I understand that number has grown. In April 2022, the FAA issued an alert to its operation managers that a commercial aircraft over West Virginia experienced a double attitude and double autopilot failure while flying under a UAP. Stigma surrounding UAP should not undermine the seriousness of this domain awareness gap.

If UAP are foreign drones, it is an urgent national security problem. If it is something else, it is an issue for science. In either case, it is a concern for safety of flight.

Next steps

To identify and evaluate the nature and intent of UAP we need (1) accurate reporting to determine scope, (2) empowered, unbiased investigation authority, (3) a transparent process to share the findings and data publicly to be studied by scientists.

Commercial pilot reporting

Today, FAA regulations direct pilots to make UAP reports to civilian organizations. Commercial aircrew who witness UAP are extremely frustrated that there is no reporting system for UAP and no protections against retaliation. They are hesitant to discuss anything "weird" on the radio with air traffic control or in any official company forum, and are only more recently talking freely amongst themselves. They are afraid of professional consequences and they deserve protection.

The absence of UAP reporting for commercial pilots creates a domain awareness gap in our airspace. If China is operating advanced UAP near Hawaii, and commercial pilots are observing it routinely, today there is no way to connect those dots.

Empowered, unbiased investigation into UAP

We need to restore decades of mistrust with the public and UAP witnesses. My lived experience over the past few months has been that as stigma is pushed back and witnesses develop trust in the process, remarkable accounts begin to emerge. The All-domain Anomaly Resolution Office is supposed to serve as a central clearing house for the analysis of UAP incidents, but it must have the authority it needs to do its job and it must build trust with witnesses. Director, Dr. Sean Kirkpatrick said in the recent NASA Independent Study Team meeting that "metallic orbs" traveling up to Mach 2 with no visible lifting surface or propulsion are being seen all over the world, but that AARO needs access to scientifically calibrated instruments to evaluate these UAP. Dr. Kirkpatrick has also indicated that eyewitness testimony SOMETHING.

We also heard him say in testimony to Congress that he only operated under Title 10 authority, and that additional authorities related to Title 50 would help AARO execute its mission. In the NASA IST public meeting he elaborated he needs access to the scientifically calibrated sensors available to the intelligence community that can characterize UAP, and my understanding is that he would need it to proactively investigate witness accounts.

However, last week, in his first public interview, he indicated he has what he needs. I am unsure why or if his statement has changed. He also indicates with respect to witnesses, that he "believes them now." I respect the challenge of the role and the obligations of a scientist to speak responsibly on this issue, but the American people want straight forward communication.

Declassification and scientific research

There are two different conversations happening regarding UAP because of overclassification of UAP data. The government has compelling UAP data that is only being disclosed in classified settings. If everyone could see the sensor and video data that I have, there is no doubt in my mind that UAP would be a top priority for our defense, intelligence, and scientific communities.

My understanding is that all UAP videos since 2021 are classified Secret or above, which prevents the American people and even some Members of Congress from seeing UAP videos like the full GIMBAL video recorded by my squadron. In the aftermath of the PRC spy balloon and the recalibration of NORAD radar filters, the American people still want to know why three UAP were shot down over several days as a threat to civilian air traffic. What were they? If they posed a threat to commercial air traffic, why is nothing else being done? The overclassification of UAP data prevents us from a true scientific investigation to get answers. The bottom line is, why are we allowing objects in our sky, particularly objects displaying advanced technology, to go unidentified? I believe we should pursue these questions about the nature of UAP with a scientific method and an open mind.

In closing, thank you for your leadership today on this important issue. The American people deserve to know what is happening in our skies. It is long overdue.

Thank you.

Commander David Fravor (Ret.)

Former Commanding Officer, United States Navy

I first want to thank you for the invitation to speak to this committee on the UAP topic that has been in the news for the past six years and seems to be continuing to gain momentum.

My name is David Fravor and I am a retired Commander in the U.S Navy. In Nov 2004, I was the Commanding Officer of Strike Fighter Squadron Forty-One, the World Famous Black Aces! We were attached to Carrier Airwing Eleven and stationed onboard the USS Nimitz (CVN-68). We were at the beginning of our workup cycle that would prepare us for a combat deployment to the Persian Gulf for operations supporting the ground forces in Iraq. The at-sea period was scheduled to go from Early November to Late December. During this period, we train with the other units in the Battle Group while integrating and honing our skills that we will rely on during our deployment.

We had been at sea for roughly two weeks, and I was scheduled to lead a 2 V 2 Air to Air training exercise. My flight of two F/A-18Fs was the Blue Air, the good guys, and we were being controlled by the USS Princeton, CG-59. Keep in mind the F/A-18F's are two-seat aircraft with the pilot in the front and the WSO (Weapons System Officer) in the back seat. The Red Air was being flown by our Marine F/A-18 squadron VMFA-232.

As we launched off the USS Nimitz, we checked in with the air controller on the USS Princeton, we were told that training was going to be suspended for real world tasking. My wingman joined up and we proceeded towards a contact to the west of our CAP (Combat Air Patrol) point. The CAP point is where we would hold prior to commencing our training runs, roughly 40 miles South of the ship.

As we proceeded to the west and as the air controller counted down the range, we had nothing on our radars and were unaware of what we were going to see when we arrived. The air controller on the ship also had no idea but had been observing these objects on their Aegis combat system for the previous two weeks. They had been descending from above 80,000 feet and coming rapidly down to 20,000 feet would stay for hours and then go straight back up.

When we arrived at the location at 20,000 feet, the controller called Merge Plot, which means that our radar blip was now in the same radar resolution cell as the contact. As we looked around, we noticed some white water off our right side. The weather on the day of the incident was as close to a perfect day as you could ask, clear skies, light winds, calm seas (no whitecaps from the waves) so the white water stood out in the large blue ocean. As all four looked down we saw a small white Tic Tac shaped object with the longitudinal axis pointing N/S and moving very abruptly over the white water. There were no Rotors, No Rotor wash, or any visible flight control surfaces like wings. As we started a clockwise turn to observe the object, My WSO and I decided to go down to get closer and the other Aircraft stayed in High cover to observe both us and the Tic Tac. We proceeded around the circle about 90 degrees from the start of our descent and the object suddenly shifted it longitudinal axis, aligned it with my aircraft and began to climb in a clockwise climbing turn. We continued down for another 270 degrees when we made a nose low move to head to where the Tic Tac would be when we pulled nose onto the object. Our altitude at this point was approximately 15,000 feet with the Tic Tac at about 12,000 feet. As we pulled nose onto the object at approximately ½ of a mile with the object just left of our nose, it rapidly accelerated and disappeared right in front of our aircraft. Our wingman, roughly 8,000 feet above us, also lost visual. We immediately turned to investigate the white water only to find that it was also gone. As we turned back towards our CAP point, roughly 60 miles east, the air controller let us know that the object had reappeared on the Princeton's Aegis SPY 1 radar at our CAP point. This Tic Tac Object had just traveled 60 miles in a very short period of time (less than a minute), was far superior in performance to my brand-new F/A-18F and did not operate with any of the known aerodynamic principles that we expect for objects that fly in our atmosphere.

We returned to Nimitz and mentioned what we had witnessed to one of my crews who were getting ready to launch. It was that crew that took the now famous approximately 90 second video that was released by the USG in 2017. What is not seen is the Radar tape that showed the jamming of the APG-73 radar in the aircraft, but we do see on the targeting pod video that the object does not emit any IR (infrared) plume from a normal propulsion system that we would expect.

What is shocking is that the incident was never investigated, none of my crew were ever questioned, tapes were never taken, and after a couple of days, it turned into a great story to tell friends. Not until 2009 did Jay Stratton contact me to investigate what we observed. Unbeknownst to all of us, Jay was part of the ATIP (Anomalous Threat Identification Program) program led by Lue Elizondo out of the DOD. I refer to the report as the Unofficial Official Report which is now available on the internet!

Years later I was contacted by Alex Dietrich, the other pilot in my flight asking if I had ever been contacted about the incident after

2009. I had since retired and my answer was no, but I told her if folks wanted to talk, I was happy to meet with them. Alex stated that she had been invited to the Pentagon multiple times to discuss the event and view other videos of UAPs. I was contacted by Mr. Elizondo shortly after talking with Alex in 2016. We briefly chatted and I was told that he would be in contact.

In the weeks that passed I was made aware that Lue had left the pentagon in protest and joined forces with Tom Delonge, Chris Mellon, Steve Justice and others to form To The Stars Academy. It was this organization that pressed the issue with leading Industry experts and USG officials, worked with Leslie Keane, Ralph Blumenthal and Helene Cooper to publish the articles in the NYT in Dec 2017 admitting the USG was looking at UAPs and removed the Stigma of the UFO topic which led to us being here today.

Those articles opened a door for the Government and the public that cannot be closed. It has led to an Interest from our elected officials who are not focused on "Little Green men" but on figuring out what these craft are, where are they from, the technology they possess, and how do they operate. It has also led to the Whistleblower protection act in the recent NDAA which brings us too today.

There are multiple witnesses coming forward that say that they have first-hand knowledge, that I'm sure Mr. Grusch will or already has discussed. What concerns me is that there is no "Oversight" from our elected officials on anything associated with our government possessing or working on craft that we believe are not from this world. This issue is not about full public disclosure that could undermine national security, but it is about ensuring that our system of checks and balances works across all work done in our government using taxpayer funds. Relative to government programs, even unacknowledged waived programs have some level of oversight by the appropriate committee members in the House and Senate and this work that is said to be occurring from whistleblower testimonies should not be exempt.

In closing, I would like to say that the Tic Tac Object that we engaged in Nov. 2004 was far superior to anything that we had at the time, have today, or are looking to develop in the next 10-plus years. If we in fact have programs that possess this technology, it needs to have oversight from those people that the citizens of this great country elected to office to represent what is best for the United States and in the best interest of its citizens.

I thank you for this time to speak with you today and God bless America!

David Grusch

Former National Reconnaissance Officer Representative, Unidentified Anomalous Phenomena Task Force, Department of Defense

Mr. Chairman, Ranking Members, and Congressmen, thank you, I am happy to be here. This is an important issue, and I am grateful for your time.

My name is David Charles Grusch. I was an intelligence officer for 14 years, both in the US Air Force (USAF) at the rank of Major and most recently, from 2021-2023, at the National Geospatial Intelligence Agency at the GS-15 civilian level, which is the military equivalent of a full-bird Colonel. I was my agency's co-lead in Unidentified Anomalous Phenomena (UAP) and trans-medium object analysis, as well as reporting to UAP Task Force (UAPTF) and eventually the All-Domain Anomaly Resolution Office (AARO).

I became a Whistleblower, through a PPD-19 Urgent Concern filing with the Intelligence Community Inspector General (ICIG), following concerning reports from multiple esteemed and credentialed current and former military and Intelligence Community individuals that the US Government is operating with secrecy—above Congressional oversight—with regard to UAPs.

My testimony is based on information I have been given by individuals with a longstanding track record of legitimacy and service to this country—many of whom also shared compelling evidence in the form of photography, official documentation, and classified oral testimony.

I have taken every step I can to corroborate this evidence over a period of four years and to do my due diligence on the individuals sharing it, and it is because of these steps that I believe strongly in the importance of bringing this information before you.

I am driven by a commitment to truth and transparency, rooted in our inherent duty to uphold the United States Constitution and protect the American People. I am asking Congress to hold our Government to this standard and thoroughly investigate these claims. But as I stand here under oath now, I am speaking to the facts as I have been told them.

In the USAF, in my National Reconnaissance Office (NRO) reservist capacity, I was a member of the UAPTF from 2019-2021. I served in the NRO Operations Center on the director's briefing staff, which included the coordination of the Presidential Daily Brief (PDB) and supporting contingency operations.

In 2019, the UAPTF director tasked me to identify all Special Access Programs and Controlled Access Programs (SAPs/CAPs) we needed to satisfy our congressionally mandated mission.

At the time, due to my extensive executive-level intelligence support duties, I was cleared to literally all relevant compartments and in a position of extreme trust in both my military and civilian capacities.

I was informed, in the course of my official duties, of a multi-decade UAP crash retrieval and reverse engineering program to which I was denied access to those additional read-ons.

I made the decision based on the data I collected, to report this information to my superiors and multiple Inspectors General, and in effect become a whistleblower.

As you know, I have suffered retaliation for my decision. But I am hopeful that my actions will ultimately lead to a positive outcome of increased transparency.

Thank you. I am happy to answer your questions.

Closing Statement

It is with a heavy heart and a determined spirit that I stand, under oath, before you today, having made the decision based on the data I collected, and reported, to provide this information to the committee. I am driven in this duty by a conviction to expose what I viewed as a grave congressional oversight issue and a potential abuse of executive branch authorities.

This endeavor was not born out of malice or dissatisfaction, but from an unwavering commitment to truth and transparency, an endeavor rooted in our inherent duty to uphold the United States Constitution, protect the American People, and seek insights into this matter that have the potential to redefine our understanding of the world.

In an era, fraught with division and discord, our exploration into the UAP subject seems to resonate with an urgency and fascination that transcends political, social, and geographical boundaries. A democratic process must be adhered to when evaluating the data and it is our collective responsibility to ensure that public involvement is encouraged and respected. Indeed, the future of our civilization and our comprehension of humanity's place on earth and in the cosmos depends on the success of this very process.

It is my hope that the revelations we unearth through investigations of the Non-Human Reverse Engineering Programs I have reported will act as an ontological (earth-shattering) shock, a catalyst for a global reassessment of our priorities. As we move forward on this path, we might be poised to enable extraordinary technological progress in a future where our civilization surpasses the current state-of-the-art in propulsion, material science, energy production and storage.

The knowledge we stand to gain should spur us toward a more enlightened and sustainable future, one where collective curiosity is ignited, and global cooperation becomes the norm, rather than the exception.

Thank you.

NOTES

1. Matt McFarland, "Elon Musk: 'With artificial intelligence we are summoning the demon,'" *The Washington Post*, December 5, 2021, https://www.washingtonpost.com/news/innovations/wp/2014/10/24/elon-musk-with-artificial-intelligence-we-are-summoning-the-demon.

2. Rory Cellan-Jones, "Stephen Hawking warns artificial intelligence could end mankind," BBC News, December 2, 2014, https://www.bbc.com/news/technology-30290540.

3. Wikipedia, s.v. "Technological Singularity," https://en.wikipedia.org/wiki/Technological_singularity.

4. "On this day—Einstein letter to FDR (October 11, 1939)," Intel Today, October 11, 2018, https://inteltoday.org/2018/10/11/on-this-day-einstein-letter-to-fdr-october-11-1939.

5. Jonathan Moeller, *The Destroyer of Worlds* (self-published, 2012), 1.

6. Graham Oppy and David Dowe, "The Turing Test," *Stanford Encyclopedia of Philosophy*, October 4, 2021, https://plato.stanford.edu/entries/turing-test.

7. Conversation with ChatGPT, generated using OpenAI's ChatGPT, 2023, https://openai.com/chatgpt.

8. Megan Garber, "When PARRY Met ELIZA: A Ridiculous Chatbot Conversation from 1972," *The Atlantic*, June 9, 2014, https://www.theatlantic.com/technology/archive/2014/06/when-parry-met-eliza-a-ridiculous-chatbot-conversation-from-1972/372428.

9. Ibid.

10. Jessica Dale, "What Is the Turing Test and Will It Ever Be Beaten?" MakeUseOf.com, April 19, 2023, https://www.makeuseof.com/tag/what-is-turing-test-ever-beaten.

11. Marshall McLuhan, *Understanding Media* (MIT Press, 1964), 80, https://mcluhangalaxy.wordpress.com/2017/07/05/marshall-mcluhan-did-predict-the-internet.

12. Miryam Brand, "The Benei Elohim, the Watchers, and the Origins of Evil," TheTorah.com, https://www.thetorah.com/article/the-benei-elohim-the-watchers-and-the-origins-of-evil.

13. Ryan Browne, "Elon Musk warns A.I. could create an 'immortal dictator from which we can never escape,'" CNBC, April 6, 2018, https://www.cnbc.com/2018/04/06/elon-musk-warns-ai-could-create-immortal-dictator-in-documentary.html.

14. Arthur C. Clarke, *Voices from the Sky: Previews of the Coming Space Age* (New York: Harper & Row, 1967).

15. Catherine Clifford, "Elon Musk: 'Mark my words—A.I. is far more dangerous than nukes,'" CNBC, March 14, 2018, https://www.cnbc.com/2018/03/13/elon-musk-at-sxsw-a-i-is-more-dangerous-than-nuclear-weapons.html.

16. Hernaldo Turrillo is a writer and author specialized in innovation. Hernaldo Turrillo, "How the Fathers of Artificial Intelligence Changed the World," IntelligentHQ, September 28, 2023, https://www.intelligenthq.com/how-the-fathers-of-artificial-intelligence-changed-the-world.

17. Jennifer Latson, "This Is Why People Think UFOs Look Like 'Flying Saucers,'" *Time*, June 24, 2015, https://time.com/3930602/first-reported-ufo.

18. Courtney Kennedy and Arnold Lau, "Most Americans believe in intelligent life beyond earth; few see UFOs as a major national security threat," Pew Research Center, June 30, 2021, https://www.pewresearch.org/short-reads/2021/06/30/most-americans-believe-in-intelligent-life-beyond-earth-few-see-ufos-as-a-major-national-security-threat.

19. Taylor Orth, "A growing share of Americans believe aliens are responsible for UFOs," YouGov, October 4, 2022, https://today.yougov.com/technology/articles/43959-more-half-americans-believe-aliens-probably-exist.

20. Robert A. Stebbins, "Aliens adored: Raël's UFO religion," *The Canadian Journal of Sociology*, September 6, 2006, https://muse.jhu.edu/article/202326/pdf.

21. Abraham Lincoln, *Abraham Lincoln papers: Series 1, Carpet Bag Papers*, 1874, https://www.loc.gov/item/mal4167500.

22. Bryce Zabel, "The 1947 Twining UFO Memo Still Matters," Medium, March 6, 2022, https://medium.com/on-the-trail -of-the-saucers/twining-memo-ufo-c719bed1d287.

23. Dr. J. Allen Hynek, "Dr. J. Allen Hynek Speaking at the United Nations, Nov. 27th 1978," UFO Evidence, http:// ufoevidence.org/documents/doc757.htm.

24. Colm A. Kelleher and George Knapp, *Hunt for the Skinwalker: Science Confronts the Unexplained at a Remote Ranch in Utah* (Pocket Books, 2005).

25. Michael Knowles, "Ex-Pentagon Official Confirms That Aliens Are Demons," YouTube, June 21, 2023, https://www .youtube.com/watch?v=NZJOXUimUSc.

26. Gary Bates, "Lifting the veil on the UFO phenomenon," Creation Ministries International, February 11, 2022, https://creation.com/lifting-the-veil-ufo-phenomenon.

27. David Ruffino and Joseph Jordan, *Unholy Communion: The Alien Abduction Phenomenon, Where It Originates and How It Stops* (Defender Publishing House, 2010).

28. Kara Goldfarb, "Serge Monast's Project Blue Beam Makes Today's Conspiracy Theories Look Sane," All That's Interesting, September 6, 2018, https://allthatsinteresting .com/project-blue-beam-serge-monast.

29. Michael Barkun, *Culture of Conspiracy: Apocalyptic Visions in Contemporary America* (University of California Press, 2014).

30. William Dever, *Who Were the Early Israelites and Where Did They Come From?* (Grand Rapids, MI: Wm. B. Eerdmans, 2003), 16.

31. Alistair McGrath, *The Passionate Intellect: Christian Faith and the Discipleship of the Mind* (Downers Grove, IL: InterVarsity Press, 2010).

32. John F. Walvoord, *The Nations, Israel, and the Church in Prophecy* (Academie Books, 1988).

33. C.S. Lewis, *God in the Dock: Essays on Theology and Ethics* (Grand Rapids, MI: Wm. B. Eerdmans, 1970), "Christian Apologetics."

34. Don Stewart, "Why Were the Books of the Old Testament Apocrypha Rejected as Holy Scripture by the Protestants?" Blue Letter Bible, https://www.blueletterbible.org/faq/don_stewart/don_stewart_395.cfm.

35. Lincoln, *Carpet Bag Papers*, https://www.loc.gov/item/mal4167500.

36. Harry S. Truman, "Statement by the President Announcing the Use of the A-Bomb at Hiroshima," Harry S. Truman Library & Museum, https://www.trumanlibrary.gov/library/public-papers/93/statement-president-announcing-use-bomb-hiroshima.

37. National Archives and Records Administration, "Project BLUE BOOK - Unidentified Flying Objects," https://www.archives.gov/research/military/air-force/ufos#usafac.

38. United States House Committee on Oversight and Accountability, "Unidentified Anomalous Phenomena:

Implications on National Security, Public Safety, and Government Transparency," July 25, 2023, https://oversight .house.gov/hearing/unidentified-anomalous-phenomena -implications-on-national-security-public-safety-and -government-transparency.

Images

Photograph of "Fat Man" Nuclear Weapon, National Archives and Records Administration, Credit: Los Alamos Scientific Laboratory, National Archives Identifier: 17553992, Local Identifier: 77-AEC-60-6282 https://catalog .archives.gov/id/175539928

Photograph of the Atomic Cloud Rising Over Nagasaki, Japan, National Archives and Records Administration, National Archives Identifier: 535795, Former Local Identifier: 208-N-43888, Local Identifier: War and Conflict Number 1242, NAIL Control Number: NWDNS-208-N-43888 https://catalog .archives.gov/id/535795

"Project Blue Book – Report No. 8, National Archives and Records Administration, Project No. 10073, 31 Dec 1952 https://i0.wp.com/prologue .blogs.archives.gov/wp-content/uploads/sites/9/2019/08/09475_2005_001 _a.jpg?ssl=1

Series: "Roswell Report Source Files" p.4 National Archives and Records Administration, National Archives Identifier: 40989309, September 23, 1947 https ://catalog.archives.gov/id/40989309?objectPage=4

Record Group 341: Records of Headquarters U.S. Air Force (Air Staff) Series: Roswell Report Source Files, National Archives and Records Administration, National Archives Identifier: 40989309, https://catalog .archives.gov/id/40989309?objectPage=9

Record Group 341: Records of Headquarters U.S. Air Force (Air Staff) Series: Roswell Report Source Files, National Archives and Records Administration, NAID: 40989309, page 23. 1949

Record Group 341: Records of Headquarters U.S. Air Force (Air Staff) Series: Roswell Report Source Files, National Archives and Records Administration, NAID: 40989310, page 6, Retrievals of the Third Kind, 1978

ABOUT THE AUTHOR

After experiencing a radical spiritual encounter at the age of seventeen, Alan DiDio was born again, instantly transforming him from a dogmatic atheist to a passionate follower of Jesus. Taught in a Word-based church, he learned early on how to stand in faith. Not long after giving his life to Christ, Pastor Alan went off to Bible college and continued serving with a national ministry for twelve years and working on staff for nearly seven. In that time, he gained experience in every possible area of ministry from running an international prayer center to traveling across the country spreading the Gospel.

Since then, he's founded Encounter Ministries and taken the Gospel to nations such as Pakistan, China, Israel, Haiti, and Guatemala. He also hosts *Encounter Today* on YouTube, which reaches millions of people around the world with the Gospel of Jesus Christ.

Pastor Alan and his wife, Tera, have two children and consider family to be the most important ministry any believer is called to.

If you'd like to connect with Alan DiDio and Encounter Ministries, visit: www.EncounterToday.com.

YOUR Prophetic COMMUNITY

Sign up for a **FREE** subscription to the Destiny Image digital magazine and get awesome content delivered directly to your inbox!

destinyimage.com/signup

Sign up for Cutting-Edge Messages that Supernaturally Empower You

- Gain valuable insights and guidance based on biblical principles
- Deepen your faith and understanding of God's plan for your life
- Receive regular updates and prophetic messages
- Connect with a community of believers who share your values and beliefs

Experience Fresh Video Content that Reveals Your Prophetic Inheritance

- Receive prophetic messages and insights
- Connect with a powerful tool for spiritual growth and development
- Stay connected and inspired on your faith journey

Listen to Powerful Podcasts that Propel You into God's Presence Every Day

- Deepen your understanding of God's prophetic assignment
- Experience God's revival power throughout your day
- Learn how to grow spiritually in your walk with God